peaceful gardens

Stephanie Donaldson

peaceful gardens

transform your garden into a haven of calm and tranquillity

RYLAND
PETERS
& SMALL
LONDON NEW YORK

For Ben

Senior designer Sally Powell

Senior editor Clare Double

Picture researcher Emily Westlake

Production Tamsin Curwood

Art director Gabriella Le Grazie

Publishing director Alison Starling

First published in the United Kingdom in 2003
by Ryland Peters & Small
Kirkman House
12–14 Whitfield Street
London W1T 2RP
www.rylandpeters.com

10 9 8 7 6 5 4 3 2 1

Text © 2003 Stephanie Donaldson
Design and photographs © 2003 Ryland Peters & Small
The following photographs © Steve Painter: 96r, 97

ISBN 1 84172 387 8

A CIP record for this book is available from the British Library

Printed and bound in China

Jacket credits:

Back jacket above: a garden in south London
designed by Roberto Silva.

Back jacket centre: Giorgio & Irene Silvagni's
house in Provence.

Back jacket below left: the garden of James
Morris in Bristol designed by Sue Berger &
Helen Phillips.

contents

6 introduction

peaceful shapes and spaces

12 keeping it simple
28 symmetry and balance
42 contemplation and relaxation
58 special places

tranquillity for the senses

72 soothing colours
82 soothing textures
98 light and shade

scent and sound

110 fragrant plants
118 herbs
128 cool water and rustling breezes

138 architects, designers and nurseries
140 picture credits
142 index

introduction

We live in a stressful world where we all need a haven, a place to forget our usual concerns – somewhere we can be simple, re-establish our place in the natural order of things and experience contentment, even if it is only for a few moments. There are people who lose themselves in books, others find physical exercise is the key, but for true contentment there is little to rival time spent in a garden. The fears and frustrations of life soon recede when there is direct contact with nature.

How you choose to spend your time in the garden is very much a matter of personal preference. It may be that you are never happier than when you are trundling along behind your lawnmower, while someone else may choose to lie in a hammock and gaze at the sky through a canopy of leaves and others will find true contentment by growing their own vegetables. Your choice will inevitably dictate your garden's appearance, but before making any changes it is always wise to separate the realizable dreams from the fantasies. The potager at Villandry is a glory to behold, but it is also extremely work intensive and the opportunities to take your ease in a garden of this kind are few and far between. However, a modest vegetable plot tucked behind a picket fence can be decorative, productive and a peaceful place. Consider carefully before you embark on creating your dream garden – small changes can be as effective as grand designs.

opposite **In a quiet corner, the soft colours of the ivy-clad wall make a backdrop to an elegant antique bench, which looks comfortably inviting with its flowery yet restrained cushions.**

A peaceful garden – simple or harmonious to look at, restful to sit in – is a place of balance, sufficiently demanding of your time to be satisfying without enslaving you. It's the place where you can be your true self, relaxed and at ease – a place where you feel free to be sad, happy or even a little sentimental. In the peaceful garden listening to the song of a bird or smelling a rose are as important as weeding; they should touch all the senses and leave you feeling enriched. In the most literal way, you can 'earth' yourself by putting your hands in the soil. So many of life's experiences today are indirect – our food often comes from the other side of the planet, the music we listen to is recorded, we communicate via telephone, fax or the internet – so when we cultivate the soil and plant a seed or seedling, nurture it and watch it grow, the wonder and satisfaction we feel are very precious.

left **An apparently carefree, informal garden demands a gardener who is happy with a degree of untidiness. To keep it in flower throughout the growing season is an endless task – far better to accept that it has its high spots and sit back and relax at other times, leaving the plants to set seed and ensure continuity in the years ahead. This style of garden is for those who work with nature rather than those who seek to control it.**

peaceful shapes and spaces

keeping it simple

symmetry and balance

contemplation and relaxation

special places

'Peace' is a word that engages heart and head – we feel it with our emotions as we understand it with our intellect. This is a central element in the creation of a successful peaceful garden. When considering any aspect of the design, check your emotional response to your plans as well as practical aspects. Remember you are seeking a calming rather than a stimulating effect.

keeping it simple

Simplicity is key. Often the starting point is what is removed rather than what is added. Taking away fussy detail and clutter and restricting the colour palette has an immediate calming effect that is both visually and emotionally satisfying. This is true of the planting as well as the solid elements contained within the garden.

below **Wide, shallow steps – the treads and margins softened by plants – lead to a mown path that curves invitingly away into the distance. Matching the width of the path to the steps creates a generous avenue for a companionable stroll.**

A garden is not just what happens within its boundaries – it is also profoundly influenced by its surroundings. Understanding these additional influences will help you create the peaceful, calming retreat you desire.

Where a garden is bordered by open countryside, distant views, other mature gardens or parkland, it should take advantage of what is known by designers as the 'borrowed view'. Allow the space to flow into its surroundings, using the landscape to lift and lead the eye to the wider view. Conversely, if buildings or unattractive features are visible from the garden, or it is enclosed by trees with no view beyond, concentrate on the inner view. Keep focal points at low levels so that the eye is engaged by what is within the garden's boundaries and does not look upwards and outwards. In either case, the eye should travel smoothly across what it sees rather than jumping from spot to spot.

When making use of the wider view, remember that it will be most effective if you resist making the garden itself too busy. Large areas of grass, some mown, some left to grow long, with a few carefully positioned trees, will lead seamlessly to the view beyond. It is no

accident that in many historic gardens the herbaceous borders and potagers are contained within walls or hedges. Their impact is all the greater when confined, and so positioned they do not detract from the surrounding landscape. In a small garden which benefits from a good view, a similar effect can be achieved by restricting borders and structures to the area

closest to the house, gradually paring down the planting and hard landscaping so that at the end of the space, adjacent to the view, the garden is at its simplest and least contrived.

Unlike the owners of the great gardens, most people who live in the country do not have a belt of parkland separating them from the more industrial aspects of agriculture – fields left

above **Concealing the labour-intensive vegetable garden behind a woven fence allows the gardener to sit and enjoy the view without being lured away from a quiet, restful moment by any task that needs doing.**

above **The tiniest garden – a windowsill, balcony or terrace – can contain miniature landscapes of great subtlety. Here, a leaf-shaped carved rock emerges from a bed of gravel. Carefully positioned succulents complete the picture.**

below **A shallow bowl emulates the arid landscape where these succulents would grow naturally.**

The mulch of pebbles is functional as well as decorative, preventing soil splashing onto the leaves during watering.

opposite **The uncluttered simplicity of this courtyard is reminiscent of a Japanese temple or a monastic cloister. The grass growing in the central stone block is the only touch of green.**

Where good views are absent, the peaceful garden needs to exclude the world beyond its boundaries. It is a more intimate and enclosed space and sometimes consists of little more than a tabletop display, a balcony or a courtyard.

uncultivated, muddy pastures or functional farm buildings – so it is generally advisable to have an informal boundary between the garden and the fields beyond. A mixed hedge of indigenous shrubs and trees works well – especially if one or two trees are allowed to grow tall and frame the view. Selective pruning of this type of boundary can work wonders (left untrimmed it is a barrier); cut lower in places to open up a view or echo the curves of the landscape beyond, it becomes part of the bigger picture.

Where a fence is necessary it is best kept low, rustic in appearance and preferably open, for example post and rail. This type of fence can always be made animal- or childproof by attaching wire netting, while still retaining the view beyond.

In less rural surroundings privacy becomes a major consideration. However fabulous the borrowed view, if it

above **A rooftop terrace is sheltered from the wind and hidden from a nearby block of flats by large-scale but simple planting that is in perfect harmony with the minimalist architecture and furniture.**

left **An urban garden keeps planting to a minimum and relies on sculptural shapes and dramatic lighting for impact – this is somewhere to look at rather than a place in which to relax. Although low maintenance, this type of garden needs regular attention to ensure the gravel stays free of fallen leaves and weeds, or it quickly looks neglected.**

opens the garden to passers-by or neighbours, some screening will be necessary or its peacefulness will be compromised. A fence topped by trellis through which plants can twine both conceals and reveals the view beyond. A tall hedge neatly trimmed into undulating curves rather than a horizontal line can be used to frame the best of the view while masking most of the garden from the outside. Seasonal screening in the shape of deciduous trees, shrubs and climbers ensures privacy in the summer months when the garden is most used, yet opens up views during the rest of the year. This type of garden can be both inward and outward looking, depending on the season.

In urban or other situations where good views are absent, the peaceful garden needs to exclude the world beyond its boundaries. It is a more intimate and enclosed space and sometimes consists of little more than a carefully arranged tabletop display, a balcony or a courtyard. Here in particular, it is the atmosphere rather than the dimensions of the garden which creates the mood. Although a barrier of trees and shrubs seems the obvious way to separate the garden from its surroundings, this can sometimes prove problematic in an urban environment. If you are overlooked by tall buildings and buffeted by gusts of wind, it may prove difficult to establish the plants, and where they do grow successfully, the result can be a dank, damp and shady garden with sour soil. In this situation the hard landscaping needs to be strong and well thought out, creating focal points and harmonious shapes that draw the eye so that the planting becomes less central. A few carefully chosen architectural plants will have far more impact and be easier to take care of than a motley selection of undemanding shrubs that is tolerant of urban conditions.

It is particularly important to relate form to function in the urban garden. However beautifully designed a garden is, if it can't be used in the way its owner envisaged, it is a failure. The conflicting emotions that result will be far from peaceful. It is important to ask yourself how you plan to make use of your garden before embarking on any changes, and any good garden designer will ask you detailed questions about what you want from your garden before redesigning it.

right **Careful pruning has revealed the sculptural shape of the tree that shades this city garden. Rather than attempting to grow other plants, which would dilute its impact and possibly struggle to survive in its shade, the designer Jonathan Bell has created textured horizontal surfaces on two levels. A simple trellis fence encloses the garden, giving it some privacy without depriving it of borrowed light. A vase of sunflowers adds a temporary splash of colour.**

Different people want different things. Some city dwellers want nothing more than a beautiful, undemanding space to look out on. They have neither the time nor the inclination to garden. They simply want somewhere that is soothing to look at at the end of a stressful day. This minimalist style of garden is very much the province of childless urbanites. A family would find that it caused more conflict than harmony when children scattered such a garden with toys or grazed their knees on raked gravel surfaces, and a keen gardener would soon grow frustrated by the lack of plants. While most people will fill a balcony or terrace with plants, others see it as an outdoor room that needs nothing more than a few carefully chosen pieces of furniture. It may irritate friends and family who long to decorate the space with plants, but if a sparsely furnished outdoor room is your idea of a peaceful garden, outsiders should not be allowed to interfere.

These days, when many of us work from home, our gardens have a new role. Any part of the garden that leads from a work space needs to be restful to look at, but not necessarily inviting or it will prove a distraction. In my own case, the view from my desk is of treetops and

above Folding chairs and a couple of rustic tables beckon invitingly, the perfect setting for a summer meal in the garden. It's tempting to imagine that the tethered goats are four-legged lawnmowers, but as they are more browsers than grazers they will probably be more interested in the food on the table.

left The curving slate wall defines and separates the different areas in this garden designed by Roberto Silva. At the far end, wooden decking creates a spacious outdoor room simply furnished with a table and chairs.

sky – good for gazing at while I think but not directly engaging. Initially I had planned to put my desk in another room where there is a view of the sea, but I realized that I would never get any work done. The ever-changing moods of the sea and the comings and goings of the fishing boats would have proved far more interesting than the task in hand. For work spaces in particular, keep the outlook simple. Avoid fussy details or planting – a single well-tended plant or tree is more appropriate than a border full of flowers that will lure you out to dead-head or prune.

When it comes to planting simplicity and restraint are more calming than busy borders incorporating single specimens of numerous varieties of plant. If you are a plant enthusiast it is easy to get carried away and end up with something that is more plant zoo than garden as you strive to include every plant that takes your fancy. When making a peaceful garden it is necessary to temper this tendency and adopt a 'less is more' approach. This is true of colour too – the use of a limited palette is more soothing to the eye than a vibrant mixture which can easily be overstimulating and is definitely not tranquil in its effect. Avoid combining colours which intensify one another and choose instead those that blend subtly together. Anyone familiar with the English countryside will know that the different shades and shapes of green that make up its meadows and woodlands create a supremely beautiful and peaceful environment. On a smaller scale this use of subtle shades rather than contrasting colours can have the same effect.

In a rural garden, using improved cultivars of the wild flowers that grow locally, in natural-looking drifts, will create a seamless blend with the countryside beyond. Cultivars select the best qualities of the wild

opposite left **Planting that echoes the local flora can link a country garden to the landscape. In this garden, large swathes of** *Geranium phaeum* **fill the foreground and pathways zigzag their way towards the graceful arching branches of a** *Buddleja alternifolia*.

opposite right **A path mown through a meadow brings you close to the beauty of the grasses without the** need to trample them underfoot. The play of light on the grass creates an ever-changing mood.

below **Inspired planting at Sticky Wicket, created by Peter and Pam Lewis. The russety-pink haze of flowering cloud grass is punctuated by the lollipop heads of** *Allium cristophii* **and pink scabious. The dried seedheads will add interest later in the year.**

Water is a wonderful addition. Keep the garden tranquil with rills that flow imperceptibly or still pools that reflect their surroundings. Keep shapes simple – rectangles, squares and circles.

flower but frequently have larger blooms and longer flowering periods. Be cautious in your use of true wild flowers unless they are from an assured source; plundering the local flora is no way to create a peaceful garden.

In a garden with large areas of lawn, a mown path can be very appealing as it curves sinuously through the long grass. The sight of long grass rippling in the wind has a quiet beauty that rivals the colourful displays of flowers in many cultivated gardens.

Leaf shape and plant outline are elements which should be considered when planning a garden. This doesn't necessarily mean that you should always seek out plants with rounded leaves and gentle curves, but that the plants you choose should enhance the atmosphere of the garden. In a minimalist garden a plant with architectural foliage is more appropriate than a rose – however beautiful the rose may be, it will look out of place and feel discordant in such a setting.

These days it seems that no garden is complete unless it has a water feature of some sort or another, and there is no doubt that, used correctly, water is a wonderful addition to a peaceful garden. A gently bubbling fountain becomes a focal point and you will become lost in a world of your own as you listen to its soothing sound and watch the movement of the water. Remember however that fast-moving water has an energizing effect, which may disrupt the contemplative mood. Avoid anything that splashes

right A rill of water flows gently across a London roof terrace in a shallow galvanized metal trough. Stones in the water echo the pebbles that surround it and a corkscrew willow casts dappled shadows.

far right Still water acts as a mirror, reflecting the surrounding trees and the sky above. Try to avoid overhanging branches though, or your pool will be filled with brown leaves in the autumn.

left **By limiting the palette of colours you use in a garden you can calm the effect of a complex planting scheme. The various shapes, shades and textures in this formal front garden create a pleasing green tapestry. Slight touches of other colours highlight the general theme. Colour-themed gardens are always most effective when other colours make subtle appearances, otherwise the effect can be dull.**

noisily or flows at a hectic pace – keep the garden tranquil with rills that flow imperceptibly or still pools that reflect their surroundings. Keep the shapes simple – rectangles, squares or circles rather than the peculiar amorphous shapes which still seem to be strangely popular. Don't forget the practicalities either. When installing water features in a garden it is always advisable to consult an expert – few things can spoil the mood of a space more effectively than a poorly installed pond that turns a murky green at the drop of a hat and requires endless maintenance. If the complexities of pumps and filters, wiring and water supplies all prove too expensive and time-consuming, you can emulate the Chinese and grow waterlilies in large, water-filled, glazed pots. Waterlilies love deep, still water and will grow happily this way, especially if they are in partial shade. Choose a small-growing or miniature variety or alternatively divide the plant every other year.

Small or large, inward or outward looking, every garden needs somewhere to sit. Bear in mind that the style of seating and the materials used for the hard landscaping should relate to the rest of the garden. Concrete paving slabs look fine in a contemporary urban garden, and decking is entirely appropriate in a waterside site, but used elsewhere they sometimes have a tendency to look uncomfortably out of place in their surroundings. When peacefulness is the aim these dissonant associations should be avoided. Seating, too, should be chosen with care – but in choosing a suitable style don't get so carried away by the aesthetic that you end up with something that is wonderful to look at but impossibly uncomfortable. Remember form *and* function – *and* simplicity.

symmetry and balance

Consider the difference between symmetry and balance within the peaceful garden. Symmetry mirrors one side of the garden with the other, while balance combines differing features in a pleasing way. Symmetry can be achieved intellectually, balance requires feeling.

left **The dark surface of the circular pond acts as a mirror, reflecting light from the sky above and creating new perspectives. Almost lost against the backdrop of the sago palm in its green planter, the flowering spike of the acanthus gains definition in the reflection.**

above **Pairs of box cones contribute to the symmetry of this formal garden. They also help lift the eye from the strong horizontals of the pond, the paving and the clipped hedges.**

Most people have a preference for either symmetry or balance. Symmetry is more ordered and predictable, balance can be fluid or curvaceous. If you are uncertain which you prefer, the photographs in this book may help you decide – do you instinctively favour formal regularity, or does a more free-form garden appeal to you? When you are deciding whether to follow the symmetrical or the balanced route it is also important to take the shape of your garden into consideration. The garden must sit comfortably within its boundaries. It is much trickier to achieve symmetry in an area which is asymmetrical in shape than in a neatly rectangular garden, and it is equally difficult to ignore the influence of the geometry on this shape of garden if you have something less formal in mind. Either way, bear in mind that your intuition is often the best guide, and it is only when something clearly isn't working that this type of analysis comes in useful.

The guiding principle of the symmetrical garden is the mirroring of one side by the other. Angles match, paths are central or flanking the centre and with the exception of the placing of a large object as a focal point at the end of a vista, this type of ornamentation is used in pairs. When it works, symmetry is emotionally and visually satisfying, but when it isn't quite right, the result can induce anxiety rather than calm – something to be avoided in a peaceful garden.

Planning helps; with the aid of a ruler and a set square (or garden design software), drawing a symmetrical garden on paper is not difficult. Even if you have never done this type of thing before you will quickly see if the proposed shapes sit well with one another. Doing this also reveals an intriguing aspect of the symmetrical garden. While it should be divided into two even halves across its width, if the same is done lengthways the proportions seldom work, nor if it is divided into quarters. If necessary, it should be divided into thirds.

left **The formality of the clipped bay trees and their wooden tubs is an interesting contrast to the rustic fencing and kitchen-garden planting of the potager beyond. Although the change of mood is apparent, the trees are evidence that although the potager may be less formal, it will still be orderly.**

right **The geometry created by the three stone balls in this Irish garden is gloriously undermined by the untrimmed nature of the copper beech hedge, resulting in a pleasing balance of formality and informality.**

It is important that paths within the garden have a destination. This may sound obvious, but it is not unusual to visit gardens where a path does nothing more than lead from the house to the fence at the end of the property. It may have access points to different parts of the garden along its way, but the lack of an arrival point can be disappointing. This is readily remedied by placing an object at the end of the path – a focal point, either modest or grand – which will draw you towards it. A beautifully planted pot, a seat to sit on and admire the view, a statue or a water feature all have the power to lure you to the furthest end of the garden.

Perspective is an important element in this type of garden and there are tricks that can emphasize this effect and make a space seem larger than it actually is. A central path that tapers as it recedes towards the end of the garden will mislead the eye into thinking that the plot is longer than it is in reality, an effect that can be enhanced by gradually reducing the size of any pots flanking the path.

far left **Flanked with topiary box balls, an antique bench is given added importance within the garden. The bench has been painted a strong shade of blue, which allows its delicate tracery pattern to stand out against the background of foliage and echo the colour of the paving.**

left **Pairs of terracotta pots planted with white daisies stand on plinths either side of a central path. Surrounded by clipped box hedging, the pots of flowers draw the eye to the ultimate destination – the pretty white-painted bench at the end of the path.**

right **There is a pleasing symmetry to this tableau. A clipped tree stands like a green parasol over a pair of painted wooden chairs and terracotta pots planted with box balls.**

above **There is a satisfying balance to the curve of this informal hedge, echoed by the gravel path and the clean-cut edge to the lawn.**

left **A curving path leads sinuously towards a half-concealed tower at the end of the garden. Low-growing bamboo lines the left-hand side of the path, while on the other side a line of large stones draws you to your destination.**

Topiary is very much at home in the formal garden – it helps emphasize symmetry far more effectively than less structured plants. Where space is restricted, topiary looks best when it is limited to no more than two different shapes, and it should always be placed in mirrored pairs or it will unsettle the atmosphere in the garden. In a large garden you have more freedom – providing the layout is strictly symmetrical, some variation in the topiary shapes can introduce a lighter mood.

Not everyone responds positively to the formal rigidity of a symmetrical garden though, even if it is softened by planting. If it all seems too contrived and ordered for your taste, you may feel more at home if your peaceful garden is a place of balance rather than symmetry. Here gentle curves define shape and contemporary materials challenge the old order, creating something new, yet still evoking a sense of restfulness in a 21st-century garden.

Although there are exceptions, the balanced garden is generally less structured than its symmetrical counterpart, with its architectural elements placed among informal planting. There are fewer obvious guidelines than in the symmetrical garden and consequently much more experimentation is called for. This approach is not suitable for anyone who is likely to fret when confronted by uncertainty.

previous page At Sticky Wicket in Dorset a precise geometry of radiating circles underlies the Impressionistic planting. To achieve such a natural-looking result requires real plant knowledge and careful management, or it could end up looking like a once-formal garden now overtaken by weeds. At the heart of the garden is a circular chamomile lawn.

left This monolithic, minimalist-style garden is not for the faint-hearted or for those who have a penchant for soft planting, but it undoubtedly has an austere beauty. Over the wall a tree attempts to break in, but within its boundaries only a small square of grass relieves a courtyard that is more about architecture than horticulture.

You may have a strong, instinctive feeling for colours and shapes that combine harmoniously, and creating a garden in this way can be a delightfully liberating affair. Free of the constraints of rules and fashion you can shape a garden that is truly yours.

The aim is to create a peaceful garden, but if you have sleepless nights as your garden evolves it becomes rather self-defeating.

If however you are attracted by this style of garden you may find that it is more difficult to visualize on paper than is a geometric design. Curves are better marked out on the ground, and when it comes to placing objects in the garden it is best to experiment with different spots until they feel right. If the object itself is too large, heavy or tall, use something more manageable that is approximately its shape and size. You can do an awful lot with a few canes and a ball of string, a chair or a stepladder and some imagination. Half-close your eyes and check the effect of the positioning on the rest of the garden – and remember to check how you feel about what you see as well as what you think.

Too often we discount intuition, but it is a very useful tool. When we look at a work of art and feel uplifted and enriched by it, we don't necessarily understand the principles of proportion or perspective or have a grasp of colour theory, but we often have a positive emotional response that is just as valid as a more informed analysis of the canvas. Similarly, you may know nothing about garden design, but have a strong, instinctive feeling for colours and shapes that combine harmoniously, and creating a garden in this way can be a delightfully liberating affair. Free of the constraints of rules and fashion you can shape a garden that is truly yours.

This is not to suggest that balance is unconstrained – far from it, think of traditional scales where all the weight starts off on one side – but the constraints are of your own devising, rather than externally imposed, and how you achieve the balance you seek is a matter of personal judgement. If this all sounds rather esoteric, it isn't. If you feel happy in your garden and there is nothing you want to change, then trust that feeling. You already have your peaceful space, regardless of the dictates of fashion or the opinions of others.

Whether your goal is a garden of balance or symmetry, you should consider its relationship with the architecture of your home and its surroundings. You may have your heart set on a wildflower garden with untrimmed mixed hedging, long grass and no visibly cultivated areas, but if the setting is a suburban street it may look more neglected than wild, causing resentment among your neighbours – and your peaceful garden will become a bone of contention rather than a place of sanctuary as intended. Similarly, a modernist house needs a garden that is sympathetic to its architecture, rather than a recreation of some earlier gardening style, or the two will rub up against one another in an uncomfortable manner. The wider view is always an important consideration.

right **Clipped squares of box give this rural garden designed by Tania Compton a formal symmetry that is made more relaxed by their planting with a mixture of roses and herbaceous perennials. In the summer flowers spill over the hedges, disguising the geometry which is more evident during the winter months.**

contemplation and relaxation

As you plan your peaceful garden it is important to remember that it is as much about how the garden is used as about how it looks – a balancing of form and function. Ideally it should be multifunctional, with open areas for family activities and entertaining as well as quiet places and hidden corners that are conducive to private contemplation.

The moods conjured up by the words contemplation and relaxation are quite different. There is a weight and seriousness, sometimes even a spiritual dimension to contemplation, which is generally thought of as a solitary activity, while relaxation is more about physical repose or socializing. To accommodate both within the same garden requires an awareness of these differences.

There is a long history of great or profound thoughts taking place in a garden, from the dawning self-awareness of Adam and Eve as they contemplated their nakedness in the Garden of Eden to Isaac Newton's formulation of the theory of gravity after he was struck on the head by a falling apple. While most of us are unlikely to change the course of history or increase scientific knowledge when we are lost in thought in the garden, we can take inspiration from historic gardens and incorporate into our own some of the elements that have long been believed to aid contemplation.

Zen, Persian, and monastic gardens all explored the meaning of life in different ways. Zen emphasizes contemplation and meditation as ways to achieve self-knowledge, and its highly symbolic gardens represent the pathway to enlightenment. The symmetry, order and symbolism of a Persian garden are an earthly representation of

above **It is easy to understand why Monet was so drawn to scenes like this – the floating flowers, the reflections, the wildlife a pond attracts all invite you to linger, observe or just relax.**

right **A vine-covered pergola shades a stone terrace where a table and chairs hold promise of alfresco meals with friends and family. At dusk lanterns light the scene, and the garden is the perfect place to be on a summer evening.**

paradise. The very word 'paradise' has its origins in Persia where the word *pardeiza* means an enclosed area. Water was the central, essential element in these gardens; it ensured fertility and cooled the air, but above all it was a metaphor for looking into the soul – as the pools of water mirrored one's image, so the garden was a place for spiritual reflection. During the Middle Ages the cloister gardens of the monastic orders were generally unadorned areas of grass, free from distraction for those who moved in prayer around

far left **With the addition of a comfortable chair this beautiful classical stone portico and its topiary sentinels overlooking a formal pond would make the perfect place to read a Jane Austen novel and dream of Mr Darcy.**

left **A wooden jetty allows close examination of a pond and its teeming life. Both practical and pleasurable, it makes the pond easier to look after and more accessible. Remove your shoes and sit on its edge dabbling your feet in the water for a perfect moment of relaxation.**

below left **A summerhouse should always be well removed from the house – a place to go to and get away from the rest of the family, to share a secret or to enjoy in solitude.**

right **Water is the great life-giver for all living things, and contemplating it is both thought-provoking and relaxing. A wildlife pond like this within a garden is beneficial for you and the environment.**

above **This charming summerhouse is a home from home with its pretty paintwork, mixture of furniture, and potted plants on the windowsills. Its appearance belies its origins as a garden shed.**

below **A length of wood tied to a rope and hung from a tree makes a simple swing – an invitation to both children and adults to stop and play.**

opposite **A Georgian-style metal bench is an appropriate choice for a** town garden. Underplanted and surrounded by lavender, with a scented climbing rose on the wall behind it and lime trees either side to create a private corner, this is the perfect spot to read a book in the sunshine or relax with a drink in the evening.

their perimeters. The physic or infirmary gardens, in which the monks grew healing plants, were places where they could contemplate their mortality as they cultivated cures to alleviate the suffering of the sick and the poor. At one end of the abbey building there was often a semi-circular garden called a paradise, which supplied flowers to decorate the altars and chapels.

Each contains elements that you may like to include in your own garden. The symbolically significant shapes and materials used in a Zen garden would be appropriate in a contemporary urban environment, the rills and reflecting pools of a Persian garden are ideal for a formal setting, while the healing herbs of a physic garden will fit in well to a country garden. In each case they will help set the mood and aid quiet thoughts.

Relaxation is less demanding – it can be found in a deckchair, on a hammock slung between two trees, lying on the grass looking up at the sky or in the company of friends sitting around a table. Anywhere, in fact, you feel comfortable enough to forget your day-to-day worries and take a bit of time out.

left **A desk with a perfect view – cool, uncluttered, conducive to thought, the scene provides restful relief from work but is not full of distraction. When working at home it is all too easy to be diverted from the matter in hand.**

above **This London roof terrace uses a screen of elaeagnus for privacy and as a windbreak, but it is not allowed to grow tall enough to obscure the view which has its own urban charm, especially at night when buildings are illuminated.**

With a little thought the same spot can be an aid to both contemplation and relaxation. Anyone who has walked around their own garden at dawn will know that the atmosphere is entirely different then to later in the day – so different that sometimes it is hard to believe that you are in the same garden. It becomes a place of mystery in the early half-light with creatures abroad that you will not see later. If you have never experienced this, it is worth making the effort – you will see the garden in a fresh light (literally) and have a sense of just how peaceful it can be.

In the same way that the garden looks different at different times of day, you can create areas which are used in a variety of ways throughout the day. A quiet moment of contemplation can be experienced standing next to a pond watching the reflections of the clouds pass across its surface, while later on it is the perfect spot in which to relax with a book. A summerhouse or pavilion at the end of the garden can be a foreign land for adventurous children, a relaxing place for a companionable tea party in the afternoon and an escape from the hurly-burly of family life in the evening. This type of building,

Try and find room for a swing. Remember when you were a child how you used to go and sit on the swing when you had something to think about? It works just as well when you are an adult.

right **A swing like this is an invitation in the landscape. Whether you picture yourself in Fragonard's painting 'The Swing' or recall when you or your children demanded to be** pushed ever higher, sitting on a swing is an evocative experience.

opposite **A simple bench on a verandah is a retreat from family life indoors.**

whether it be summerhouse or shed, pavilion or temple, should be situated far enough away from the house to ensure that it fulfils its function as a refuge. Too close and you will be tempted back into domesticity, or it will become an annexe of the house with everyone congregating there just when you try to snatch a quiet moment.

In the centre of old Amsterdam in Holland, all the 17th-century houses that line the canals of the Grachtengordel have garden houses at the farthest point from the house. Some are grand stone affairs with intricate carvings and marble floors, others are built from wood with decorative fretwork embellishments, while elsewhere the tradition continues with modern buildings beyond the flower-filled gardens. The uses of the buildings are as varied as the styles of their architecture, but what they have in common is that they are removed from the influence of domestic life and as such can be used as places of refuge.

Treehouses have traditionally been children's territory, but increasingly adults are having them built for themselves. Very different from the dens fashioned from old planks and crates that I remember from my childhood, some are proper rooms

left **The curve of this hammock perfectly echoes the contour of the arch above it, but the unforgiving stone beneath is not ideal. It may be better to hang a hammock above grass or some other soft surface.**

perched in trees like the Swiss Family Robinson's treetop eyrie, with chairs and tables, beds and even electricity and running water in some instances. Others restrict themselves to being lofty lookouts, but either way, they offer a perfect opportunity to relax and recapture the excitement of childhood adventures.

So, too, do swings and hammocks; after all relaxation is as much about fun as it is about rest, so even if children don't regularly use your garden, try and find room for a swing – not a modern, playground swing but something old-fashioned to hang from a tree. Visiting children will be delighted and it is guaranteed to be well used by adults, too. Remember when you were a child how you used to go and sit on the swing when you had something to think about? It works just as well when you are an adult. Hammocks are a source of entertainment as well as ultimate relaxation. The entertainment is to be had from watching others trying to get into the hammock without falling out; sitting up in a hammock is neither easy nor recommended. The relaxation comes when they succeed. Sling a hammock in a secluded corner of the garden where you will be left undisturbed.

Finding peace and quiet in the city is a far harder prospect, but roof gardens, balconies and terraces do lift you above the hustle and bustle

contemplation and relaxation **53**

right A simple wooden
bench tucked away in
the corner of this building
offers privacy, concealment
or shelter from the rain.

far right A suitably rustic
chair and table blend in
perfectly in this woodland
clearing. Made from robust
materials, they can be left
out all year round so that
they are always available
for an impulse visit.

and provide an outside space for those who
spend most of their lives indoors. The ideal
arrangement in this type of raised urban garden
is a low screen of planting that gives shelter and
privacy when you are sitting down but does not
obscure the view. In the absence of countryside,
this sense of space is a valuable commodity and
becomes a beautiful sight when lit at night.

An old-fashioned verandah or a terrace next
to the house may provide the occasional quiet

moment for contemplation early in the morning
or in the evening, but its primary function is as
an informal gathering place. It is usually
positioned to make the best of the climate.
Sheltered, sometimes shady and certainly
convenient, it is where family and friends
get together for alfresco meals, to exchange
confidences or enjoy a siesta in a comfy chair.
Pots of favourite plants often find a home
here, and tending them, especially if they are

left **These days treehouses are as likely to be built for adults as for children. Either way they are a perfect place to get another perspective on the garden – or even life! Before you build, you should check with your neighbours if it overlooks their garden, and in some areas planning permission is required.**

opposite above **Removable covers and synthetic fillings are best for outdoor cushions. If they are left out overnight they can be washed and dried without permanent damage.**

opposite below **A quiet bench well away from the house is a refuge from interruptions, ringing telephones and all the other demands of life. It's a place to think, to dream or catch up on your reading (although a cushion or two might be advisable).**

sweetly scented, is a relaxing pastime for those who find
it hard to sit down for long.

A garden that is used for contemplation and relaxation
needs plenty of places to sit. These include solitary chairs
in secluded corners where you can think deep thoughts,
benches in sunny spots surrounded by scented plants where
you can exchange confidences or sit in companionable
silence, and folding chairs that can be easily moved to take
advantage of a patch of sun or shade depending on the
season. Seats carefully positioned around the garden will
reveal the best views to visitors, or encourage them to pause
alongside a pond or other garden feature that is worthy of
closer examination. Comfortably cushioned chairs in a
summerhouse might persuade you to take shelter there
instead of retreating indoors during summer showers – there
is something delightfully frivolous about sitting somewhere
like this waiting for the rain to stop instead of rushing inside.

Eating outdoors is one of life's great pleasures, providing
that it is a comfortable experience. Ideally the table and chairs

should be close to the kitchen – that way it's
easy to be spontaneous and decide on the spur
of the moment to decamp outside. The idea of
eating at the far end of the garden may appeal,
but the reality is that someone has to carry
everything there and back, a chore that is not
always conducive to domestic harmony. Have an
occasional picnic there instead and leave the
table and chairs somewhere more convenient.

Because it needs to withstand the weather,
most garden furniture is a compromise between
comfort and durability, which means that a good
supply of cushions is essential. Keep a large
basket of them in the porch, summerhouse or
shed so that they are easy to bring out and put
away. Make sure they are washable, and if you
live somewhere where the winters are cold or
damp, bring the cushions indoors and store
them in a warm place or they will become
musty. Small details like these may seem rather
trifling, but when they are a cause of irritation or
argument they can interfere with the peaceful
atmosphere of the garden.

special places

Within every garden there are places that are invested with meaning, places where an object, a plant or a view has particular significance for the gardener. It can be a memento recalling love or loss, a work of art or a even a tree grown from a seed.

What makes a place special? It is your relationship with that place and how that connection was forged. Maybe it brought you comfort in adversity, calm when all around was in turmoil or joy in a troubled world. But it need not be the big experiences of life that make this link, sometimes it is the private pleasures: finding the first snowdrop in midwinter, watching a fledgling fly or picking and tasting the first peas you have ever grown – simple things that can tie you to a particular spot in the garden. When life gets complicated you can go to that special spot, or visit it in your imagination and feel comforted.

right **A door left ajar is an invitation to explore further. There is always a sense of excitement and anticipation about what might lie beyond.**

opposite left **A spiral of flints gathered from within this Dorset garden and laid on the moss-covered ground draws you in to its heart. Through the year this space, designed by Ivan Hicks, retains its special quality – cool refuge in summer, intriguing land art in winter.**

opposite right **A modern London garden by Roberto Silva undergoes a change of mood when it is briefly transformed by a carpet of pink cherry-blossom petals.**

right **In a Beverly Hills garden, weathered balustrading reclaimed from Rudolph Valentino's home Falcon's Lair is used to great effect as the railings for an atmospheric walkway that leads to a summerhouse at the bottom of the garden.**

A special space can be something private and exclusive to you or a shared experience. When it is shared it can be a way of communicating to others how you feel about them or your garden, but be discriminating about who you choose to do this with or you may risk spoiling the place or the relationship.

It may be that your special space needs no embellishment, but sometimes it is nice to celebrate the relationship by adding your own decorative touches to an otherwise low-key spot. 'Found' objects gathered from around the garden often work best; they have an integrity and a rightness that can be missing from imported materials. This type of decoration is reminiscent of the cave paintings, dolmens and menhirs of our earliest ancestors.

On the other hand, a work of art by a favourite artist may find a perfect home in your special place. It can be fitting to mark an unexpected windfall or work well done with this type of memorial. Make sure whatever you add has some significance, or it will be little more than furniture – filling the space but adding nothing to its meaning. Works of art, when appropriate, give structure to a place and act as anchor points that focus the attention. Over time their

left **In the garden of Mirabel Osler, a mirrored archway creates the illusion of another garden – the ultimate special space – visible but not attainable. By angling the mirror so that it is not approached straight on the illusion is sustained. Keep it clean though, or it will fool no one.**

below **The beauty and dignity of a sculpture of this quality will never pall. A treasured memento of travel to a faraway place, it also acts as a reminder of happy times. Such a fine work of art is a very special addition to a garden and needs to be carefully positioned.**

beauty changes and transforms as they become weathered and they settle into their surroundings.

If works of art are beyond your means or do not appeal, there are several less costly alternatives worth considering. Reclamation yards are filled with all manner of extraordinary items in all sorts of materials, from broken columns to old metalwork, which can add character and a sense of history to your garden. Sometimes a stroll around one of these will present you with the perfect object at a knock-down price.

Mirrors can be used to create the illusion of a larger space or another garden through an arch or doorway, especially if the mirror is slightly angled so that visitors do not see their reflections as they approach it. Mirrors also bring light to otherwise dark areas, similarly stained-glass panels positioned so that the sun can shine through the jewelled colours will transform a space into something utterly magical.

One of the most seductive features in a garden is a door in a wall. It harks back to childhood and the world of the imagination conjured up by books like *The Secret Garden* by Frances Hodgson Burnett and the Narnia stories by C. S. Lewis. Some years ago I had the experience of being lost in the depths of the Somerset countryside; arriving at the outskirts of an unknown village I stopped next to a wall to get my bearings. Looking up from my map I noticed a door in the wall which bore the simple legend 'To the Garden'. Feeling like a character from *Alice in Wonderland* I felt compelled to

Works of art give
structure to a place
and act as anchor
points that focus the
attention. Over time
their beauty changes
and transforms as they
become weathered
and they settle into
their surroundings.

opposite left **Garden art does not need
to be effective. This wind
chime was made by suspending flattened
spoons and an old bell from fishing line.**

opposite right **Designer Ivan Hicks created
a woodland work of art by piling a cairn of
stones on top of a reclaimed stone frame.**

right **A magnificent urn fashioned from
slate by sculptor Joe Smith is an object
of wonder as well as something of great
beauty. It needs no embellishment and the
surrounding planting has rightly been kept
at a low level.**

far left An arching pair of rustic poles marks the beginning of a grassy path winding through a wildflower meadow and perfectly frames the distant tree, which might otherwise go unremarked.

left The rustic poles at the edge of the meadow echo the shape of the archway that leads from the garden, drawing you forward to explore what lies beyond.

investigate, excited yet also a touch fearful of what I might find beyond. I'm pleased to report that I neither fell down a well nor encountered the Red Queen. Instead I found myself in the garden that had once belonged to the great plantswoman, Margery Fish – a memorable visit that has forged a special relationship between me and that place.

Simple touches are often more effective than grand decorative flourishes. When framing a view, it is the view, not the frame, that should draw the attention. The frame provides an appropriate setting, but if it is unnecessarily elaborate it will act as a distraction. Subtlety deepens the experience. A curving path that leads you on to a unseen destination, a half-hidden wicket gate in a hedge, a door left ajar in a wall – all invite exploration, and the pleasure and surprise at the discovery of a wonderful view or a hidden garden is all the greater for the journey that has been taken. A sense of mystery enlivens a garden and promises revelation.

Plants too make a vital contribution to a special space. They can be used to enclose, conceal, frame or surround your chosen spot.

left At the end of this path a quirky, homemade fence and arch give the furthest part of the garden a sense of enclosure without totally concealing the space from the rest of the garden. A solid fence would make the garden feel smaller.

opposite A grass pathway, its margins softened by plants, leads to a wooden doorway, tempting you to explore further. Even if the door does not conceal a hidden garden, by its very existence it makes the space seem bigger.

Their colours, textures and fragrances help define and emphasize the mood. A shady garden can be enlivened by drifts of white flowers that bring light and contrast – a wooded glade becomes romantic when softly illuminated by white foxgloves and martagon lilies. A sunny corner, where fragrant lavender and rosemary surround a stone seat and creeping thymes grow among the flagstones, will be filled with colour and a heady fragrance. Climbing plants that are allowed to clothe a wall and curtain an archway offer both concealment and discovery. Sometimes a single plant is all you need, especially in a contemporary minimalist garden – a rustling bamboo that moves gently in the wind, an architectural plant that throws dramatic shadows on a painted wall, a solitary tree to soften the stones that surround it. The right plant in the right place.

Sometimes it is the plants themselves which make the space special – it might be a rose grown from a cutting from your childhood garden, a souvenir of a lovely holiday or a tree raised from a seed by one of your children who has now grown up and left home. Plants like this

are loaded with significance and create a living bond between you and your garden.

My own garden is full of such plants and when I walk around it I find myself reliving the experiences and thinking of friends and family. There is the olive tree I bought back from Tuscany as a sapling, now ten feet tall; a blue perennial cornflower known by all the family as 'Mrs. Bottomley' in honour of the person who gave us the first small plant from her garden, and most significantly for me, a perfect, richly scented pink rose, reputedly grown from a cutting taken from a rose that grew on the poet Omar Khayyam's grave. I planted it originally in the garden of the first home I lived in as an adult and when I moved it was potted up and moved with me. It then spent twenty years in that pot moving from place to place, and it is only now that I have at last found my special space that I feel ready once more to plant it in my garden.

opposite **An old stone column hints at the possibility of an earlier, more formal garden, lost long ago. The trimmed topiary counterpoints the air of abandon, showing that the effect is intentional.**

above left **A doorway in a wall is the most romantic of entrances to a garden.**

below left **A beautifully simple wooden bench carved with a couple's initials transforms this wooded glade into a trysting place.**

tranquillity for the senses

soothing colours

soothing textures

light and shade

Detail is as important in the peaceful garden as design and layout. Choosing the right colours and textures and observing the effect of light and shade help set the mood. Let your emotions be your guide – if a colour, a texture or a play of light calms and pleases you it will contribute to the overall effect of the garden.

soothing colours

The peaceful garden requires a subtle and restrained palette, where plants blend in harmonious drifts. Cool, soft, or pastel colours will complement the calm mood.

The gentle, soothing presence of green is at the core of the peaceful garden. The myriad shades of the foliage forms the backdrop and supplies the supporting cast for the flowers, their delicate beauty becoming all the more apparent when set in a sea of green. It is a constantly metamorphosing colour, from the fresh acid greens of spring through the dusky greens of summer to the transformations of autumn and the rich, glossy leaves of evergreens and glaucous hues of conifers in winter. In his poem 'The Garden', the poet Andrew Marvell (1621–1678) wrote of 'a green thought in a green

shade'. Nearly four hundred years later we still feel the pull of that phrase, and like Marvell will often seek out a cool, bosky corner of the garden in which to think quiet thoughts.

In the peaceful flower garden too, green often predominates, while the other colours which feature are chosen to be complementary rather than contrasting. Whites, creams, pinks, blues and purples all blend together harmoniously, and soft yellows have their place as well, but contrasting colours such as oranges, bright reds and bright yellows should be avoided as they intensify the greens and

above **The starburst flower heads of alliums last many weeks in the garden and the seedheads that follow are just as decorative, if not quite so colourful.**

left **In early spring it is unusual to see pink flowers; the blooms of this alpine clematis (*Clematis macropetala*) are an exception.**

opposite **At the foot of a hedge the long grass is left untrimmed to allow the alliums and cow parsley to bloom undisturbed. The colour of the alliums is just a shade darker than the flowers on the Judas tree (*Cercis siliquastrum*).**

right The intense blue of morning glory is one of the most appealing colours in the garden, and the transience of the flower adds to its beauty.

below As flowers develop from bud to fully opened flower their colours change; the cerise of this unfurling allium will soften with age.

opposite The flowering habit of the colourful and unusual *Primula vialii* resembles that of a wild orchid with its succession of tiny flowers opening over many weeks. The rust-coloured cone at the top of the flower head conceals the unopened buds.

make the effect less calming. A garden with little or no foliage, or one where foliage is secondary to the flowers, may have impact, but it is seldom peaceful in its mood. Think of the bulb fields of Holland where great gashes of colour transect the landscape, or carpet bedding schemes with their hectic patterns – both attract attention, but neither soothes the eye.

If this all sounds rather too wishy-washy for your taste, don't despair. Although the palette may be restricted, the range of shades is not, and there is plenty of opportunity to use wonderfully rich colours. Combining deep shades of purple and pink with strong blues creates an intensely colourful tapestry, and softer plantings always look more interesting when some dark tones are included.

Weaving the plants among one another blends the colours like an Impressionist painter. This is most easily done by planting in irregular-shaped drifts that consist of uneven numbers of plants – three, five or seven for example. This effect can work well even in a formal garden.

PICTURES OVERLEAF
above left Although not quite as vigorous as its green cousin, the rich, dark colouring of purple basil makes it worth growing.

below left The canna lily is a tender plant, but nurture it for the striking colours of its architectural leaves and its bright flower spikes.

centre **The steely blue flowers of** *Eryngium bourgatii* **have an appealing thistle-like quality. In the evening light their colour appears to deepen and they stand out from their surroundings.**

right **Walking along this grassy path, lined with the soft colours and heady fragrance of the marjoram (***Origanum***), cotton lavender (***Santolina***) and catmint (***Nepeta***), is guaranteed to be a sensory pleasure.**

above far left **Ammi majus is a delicate, cultivated form of cow parsley usually grown as a hardy annual.**

above centre **The shades of Astrantia major range from white to pink and red. Grow in light shade where the paler colours show up well.**

above left **The foxglove Digitalis purpurea f. albiflora is a stately presence in a border or woodland garden.**

below far left **These white agapanthus make excellent container plants in full sun.**

below centre **White flag iris flower briefly but beautifully.**

below left **Flowering grasses such as Eriophorum angustifolium have a subtle beauty.**

FLOWERS FOR SOOTHING COLOURS

Agapanthus

Allium

Ammi majus (bishop's flower)

Astrantia major (masterwort)

Cerinthe

Clematis macropetala (alpine clematis)

Digitalis purpurea f. *albiflora* (white foxglove)

Eryngium bourgatii (sea holly)

Helleborus orientalis (hellebore)

Hesperis matronalis (sweet rocket)

Hydrangea

Ipomoea (morning glory)

Iris

Lavandula (lavender)

Nepeta (catmint)

Nigella (love-in-a-mist)

Origanum (marjoram)

Papaver somniferum (opium poppy)

Box edging or other features provide the structure and definition for the soft planting within. Such planting, however, is not suited to a symmetrical arrangement and can easily look messy, especially if a plant or two fails and leaves the whole display looking somewhat gap-toothed.

Colour-themed gardens are popular and they can be very restful. The White Garden at Sissinghurst is a good example – with its white, silver and grey plants, it is a serene and inspiring place to sit. Even though the palette is restricted there is an enormous variety of subtly different colours which blend together to create the overall picture. Rigid adherence to the stated colour theme creates blandness in the garden, and neurosis in the gardener!

Depending on the time of day, colours can look very different – blues and whites tend to look harsh or washed out at midday, yet at dawn and dusk they take on a luminous quality that is quite hypnotic in its effect. This type of transformation is at the heart of the peaceful garden.

far left **A green-painted bench echoes the colour of the surrounding foliage and the grass beneath it. This subtle coloration is ideal for a peaceful garden.**

left **Ferns such as this** *Dryopteris dilatata* **are perfect plants for a shady woodland garden.**

below **A leafy path edged with hedges and overhung by trees draws you deeper and deeper into the garden. There is no need for any colour except green in this type of setting.**

right **The brilliant green of young shuttlecock fern (***Matteuccia struthiopteris***) fronds unfold in a consummate display of natural beauty.**

soothing textures

Every plant and every surface within the garden has a texture and a relationship with its surroundings. Soothing textures are more about that relationship than the feel of a leaf or the finish of a stone.

An easy way to understand the relationship between different textures is to look at a Zen garden. Its timeless and peaceful beauty is an enduring legacy of the Buddhist monks who created it. By creating symbolic gardens that represented the pathway to enlightenment, the monks were able to explain the principles of Zen to their followers.

Each rock, tree or shrub is placed with infinite care and has special meaning. A rock placed horizontally can represent the sky, vertically the earth, or depending on shape or position, it may be an island or even an

above **The gentle curve and smooth finish of the timber deck contrasts pleasingly with the varied textures of the rough slate and mixed stones. A carpet of cherry blossom petals adds a temporary softness to the composition.**

above left **There is a pleasing juxtaposition of materials and textures in this picture – a wooden deck gives way to concrete steps and a low wall that leads onto concrete stepping stones. The hard surfaces are made less brutal by the rounded stones that surround them, and a grassy plant softens the setting further.**

above right **The smooth textures and linear design of the etched glass window and plain panelled walls are emphasized by decking, laid at right angles to the building. Everything changes when the deck meets stones.**

below **Sometimes all you need to highlight texture is a variation in size.**

animal. A clipped shrub symbolizes billowing clouds and the use and form of small pebbles, gravel and sand help create an atmosphere conducive to meditation.

Each element is pared-down, simple and refined. Change is not necessary. There is nothing superfluous or frivolous, no giving way to the temptation to include a favourite flower or put a seat in a sunny corner. In the Zen garden everything has added meaning and looking at it can be a profound experience.

This doesn't mean that every peaceful garden should follow the Zen model, but it can help you to reach an understanding of how to combine elements successfully when you mix planting and hard landscaping. Once more this is an aspect of garden design which needs to involve your emotional response. If the juxtaposition of two different textures feels right then it usually is; if, on the other hand, you feel uncomfortable, then maybe you need to try some other solutions.

The obvious way to check how you react to textures is to touch them. Hold a smooth stone in your hand and notice how you turn it round and round, pick up a handful of gravel and pour it from one hand to the other, run some sand through your fingers – these are tactile experiences and will help you understand how you relate to the materials. Not all responses are positive; some people hate sand (it reminds them of gritty sandwiches on the beach), while others dislike gravel surfaces because they love to walk barefoot in the garden. By exploring your responses to the different textures before you embark on your garden you can create an environment tailored to your own preferences.

PLANTS FOR SOOTHING TEXTURES

Artemisia 'Powis Castle' – ferny foliage

Ballota pseudodictamnus – woolly foliage

Bamboos – ferny foliage

Eryngium alpinum – tickly/prickly, ferny leaves

Eschscholzia (California poppy) – silky petals and ferny foliage and flowers

Ferns – curling fronds

Foeniculum vulgare (fennel) – ferny foliage

Hosta – bold, ribbed leaves

Papaver somniferum (opium poppy) – silky flowers and ferny foliage

Pelargonium tomentosum – hairy, ferny foliage

Romneya coulteri – papery flowers and ferny foliage

Salix caprea (pussy willow) – velvety catkins and bold foliage

Salvia officinalis (sage) – bold, rough leaves

Sedum – bold, fleshy leaves

Stachys lanata – bold, woolly leaves

Stipa tenuifolia – hairy

Thalictrum – ferny foliage

Verbascum olympicum – bold, woolly leaves and flower spikes

But the peaceful garden does not consist solely of rounded stones and velvety leaves. It is the relationship of one thing with another that is important, and here a contrast often works better than textures or shapes that are too similar. Think of a border where all the plants have similar leaves, or a garden where every surface is the same – the effect is more likely to be boring than soothing.

There are words which describe texture or shape that have the power to soothe – words like round, curved, smooth, undulating. They can be used as guides to some of the textures to include in your garden, especially the surfaces – paving, steps, walls and water features. The materials that are used for these elements in the garden are most successful when they are sympathetic to their surroundings. Polished concrete, slate and metal are perfectly at home in an urban setting, while rustic timber, weathered brick and stone blend seamlessly into a country garden. This sensitivity to the surroundings is part of what makes a garden peaceful – jarring notes should be avoided. Imagine a country garden where a blue glass mulch has been spread on a border, or a city garden where a cottage garden arch, complete with roses, is placed in minimalist surroundings. Eccentric maybe, but definitely not soothing.

The materials traditionally used for building in your area can also be used as a guide. If the houses are built of granite, a garden that features sandstone will look out of place – think of the two materials alongside one another and it will give you an idea of whether your

left **This pared-down urban terrace where textures dominate and plants take a back seat requires no more than a couple of hours of maintenance a year. A simple square trellis encloses the area and the few plants that grow against it focus the eye inside the garden. Irregular-shaped blocks of York stone are bedded in smooth pebbles. The terrace is edged with concrete which has a sunken recess for a barbecue or fire.**

right **There is a monumental feeling to this stone wall with its rough-hewn surfaces. Built solely as a blockwork wall it would feel imprisoning, but intersected by the pillars of stone it becomes far more significant. Any plants would detract from its power, and the simple grass carpet seems entirely appropriate.**

choice is appropriate. In this instance, slate looks much better with granite than sandstone. When the material is right, its texture becomes less significant. And once the hard landscaping has been resolved, it becomes much easier to choose suitable plants.

There are as many plant textures as there are plants; the differences, sometimes obvious, sometimes subtle, are as important as the variation of colour within a garden. Read through a list of plant descriptions and texture is a key element, whether soft and hairy, plump and fleshy, deeply ridged, prickly, fuzzy or thorny. You will respond to the texture as much as you do to the other details.

When walking around the garden notice how often your hand reaches out to touch a flower, stroke a leaf or feel the smoothness of bark. Your brain may not always register what you are doing, but in the same way that stroking a pet induces calm, this tactile tour of the garden is a soothing experience. In most gardens the plant textures are incidental, but when you are making a peaceful garden you can consciously select your favourite surfaces, barks or patinas. They will sustain the garden long after flowers have faded. In the same way that the blending of colours creates patterns in the garden, so the combining and blending of textures gives rhythm and variation to the planting.

Viewed from a distance, texture is about shape and outline – after all touch cannot be experienced from afar. But interesting outlines and contrasting shapes will draw you closer until you are near enough for a

far left **Bluestone and pink bricks compose this small, square, textured terrace, leading to a gravelled area.**

left **An informal path has steps made from salvaged railway sleepers and gravel. Plants grow happily in the gravel, softening the edges and self-seeding readily.**

above **The curled tips of hosta leaves push through a seemingly hostile environment of pebbles and stones. At present the hard landscaping is more evident than the plant, but once the hosta leaves are open they will dominate.**

right **This is a garden full of contrasting textures, not all of which combine happily. A decking boardwalk leads across a dry garden of bold, linear plants such as palms, grasses and phormiums. Behind this carefully set scene a conventional garden intrudes rather uncomfortably.**

above **This wall, made from Welsh slate using drystone walling techniques, is both beautiful and practical. It snakes its way through the garden dividing different areas, its rough texture a contrast to its curving shape.**

right **Different hard landscaping materials make an interesting pattern on this garden floor. In the foreground the linear planks, set in stones, draw you further into the garden, where the curving sets lead you to either side of the central area laid with simple paving slabs.**

90 tranquillity for the senses

above left **Like fragments of lost paving from an ancient ruin these carefully placed stones, set among pebbles, have much more presence than conventional paving.**

above right **This patterned path in a herb garden has a wonderful patina of age. Natural materials such as stone, brick and tile age beautifully and become more subtle as years pass.**

truly tactile experience. This is where texture becomes really significant. Surfaces – of leaves, stems, bark, fruit and even flowers – gain their character as much from their texture as their colour, and in gardens where colour is restricted, texture is essential to avert monotony. Describe a leaf as puckered, ribbed, rough, smooth, shiny, matte, prickly, thorny or furry and you quickly realize how very different they are one from another, not just in appearance but in the effect that they have on the general view. Shiny surfaces advance, appearing closer than they actually are, while matte finishes have the opposite effect and tend to recede.

There are three basic shapes of foliage in the garden – bold, linear and ferny. Bold encompasses the big leaves like *Fatsia*, *Gunnera*, *Rheum* and *Hosta*; these sorts of leaves are popular in tropical or architectural planting schemes. Linear includes sword-like foliage and many of the grasses, while ferny covers the softer shapes including, of course, ferns. By combining these shapes in your planting you create instant interest. If you still find it difficult to grasp the impact that texture has on planting, try taking black-

and-white photographs of your garden. By removing the distraction of colour, texture comes to the fore. If the pictures all look rather monotonous this is an indication that you need to introduce more contrasting textural effects.

Bold foliage plants bring substance to the garden, but scale and proportion also need to be considered. Including the grandest of these plants in a small garden can leave room for little else – fine if it is a simple, minimalist garden, but very limiting if it is not. Also bear in mind that some plants, such as *Gunnera*, die right down in winter, leaving very little evidence of their otherwise impressive presence. On a smaller scale, hostas provide some of the best bold foliage in the garden. Their large ridged, pleated or puckered leaves have a wonderful textural quality and the colour variations add further interest. They too have their limitations – they are a favourite food of slugs and snails, and their beautiful leaves can be reduced to lace where these pests are a problem. In such cases hostas are best grown in pots protected by copper tape or another deterrent.

Although not all linear plants are grasses they make up by far the largest group of plants, encompassing everything grassy from giant bamboos to the prettily compact *Festuca glauca*. Grass, in all its shapes and forms, provides many of the most soothing

above left *Stipa gigantea* is the stateliest of grasses. From its base it sends up a spectacular fountain of tall flowering stalks which turn golden bronze during summer.

above centre *Briza maxima* is commonly known as quaking grass, a perfect name for this delicate annual with ever-moving pendent seedheads. Their appearance invites you to run your fingers through them.

above right The bronzy-red leaves and large panicles of delicate purple flower heads of *Panicum virgatum* 'Shenandoah' make this a particularly appealing switch grass.

opposite *Stipa tenuissima* is one of the most tactile grasses, with its soft green hairlike foliage tinged bronze at the tips. Its texture is reminiscent of doll's hair. The shape and texture of the grass contrasts nicely with the knapweed.

textures in the garden. And not just the ornamental varieties either – think of your lawn and the pleasure to be gained from walking on it barefoot, or lying on your back looking up at the sky. Both are highly evocative experiences, often sending you back to your childhood and more carefree times. If you haven't done either in a long time, you are missing out on two of the simplest, purest pleasures to be found in the garden.

In recent years ornamental grasses have become increasingly popular with gardeners as informal planting has taken over from the ordered borders of the past. The relaxed, fluid effect of grasses is perfectly at home in contemporary gardens, whether they are in an urban or rural setting. The fact that they are very easy to grow, undemanding and look wonderful throughout the year has also helped their popularity. Even in the dead of winter the dry stems and seedheads have a presence in the garden, especially when they are rimed with frost. They are important for wildlife too – beneficial insects hibernate among the dry foliage and birds find valuable food in the seedheads. Leaving the grasses untrimmed fits in well with their correct care. They should be cut back, thinned or divided in spring rather than in the autumn. This will prevent them rotting, usually caused by water getting into the crown.

opposite **The cat's-tongue roughness of sage leaves does not appeal to everyone.**

this page **Succulent plants beg to be touched. From the smallest to the largest, their fleshy leaves have an irresistible tactile quality. They store** moisture in their foliage so will grow happily in arid conditions such as the tops of gateposts, or in shallow containers on tabletops. With their modest demands they could easily be overlooked, but close study reveals fantastic variations in colour and texture.

above **Before young hosta leaves have opened fully the contrasting colour and texture of their undersides is attractively revealed. Noticing these gradual transformations is one of the pleasures of the peaceful garden.**

right **Droplets of water hang on the ferny foliage of a fennel plant. Touching the plant when it is wet is a very different, not necessarily enjoyable experience, compared to running your fingers through it when it is dry.**

The third basic shape – ferny – naturally includes many ferns. Some ferns will grow happily in dry shade or other difficult situations and their delicate fronds contrast softly with the other, more architectural shapes. In sunny, open positions other plants with fern-like foliage are more appropriate – *Thalictrum*, *Artemisia*, *Eschscholzia*, and *Senecio cineraria* are just a few examples.

It is useful to have lists of plants that fit into the different categories when you are planning your garden. One of the best ways to compile such a list is to visit a good garden centre and make a note of anything that appeals to you

Hostas provide some of the best bold foliage in the garden. Their large ridged, pleated or puckered leaves have a wonderful textural quality and the colour variations add further interest.

under the three headings bold, linear and ferny. Not only will this broaden your plant knowledge, but you will also have a clearer understanding of the different shapes, which are just as relevant whether you are looking at a tiny alpine or a 5m (16ft) bamboo.

As you make your choices, other categories and sub-categories will also become evident, and this is where texture really comes into play. Woolly-leaved plants like *Stachys lanata*, also known as lamb's or rabbit's ears, are irresistible – stroking their leaves is reminiscent of the feel of a favourite stuffed toy from childhood – while the tall mullein, *Verbascum olympicum*, has huge, bold, woolly leaves and flower spikes that bear golden flowers. While you are making your list, notice the plants that you touch and be sure to make a note of them too. Roses may be prickly, but their flower petals feel like silk. Sedums are usually bought for their bright autumn flowers and their ability to attract butterflies, but their cool, fleshy leaves are good to touch. Fennel is thought of as a culinary herb, but its ferny foliage looks wonderful in the flowerbed too, and brushing against it is pleasantly tickly. The textures in a peaceful garden are as much about the tactile experience as they are about their appearance.

left The delicate unfurling leaves of the aptly named hart's-tongue fern *Asplenium scolopendrium* do not have the usual ferny foliage of the genus. Their shiny, rather leathery leaves have a strong linear quality.

left **Strong light tends to bleach all but the most vibrant colours. In this garden shade is welcome not just because of the coolness it provides, but also because it is restful on the eyes.**

right **The variegated leaves of a yucca are given further interest by the play of light and shade on the plant and its surroundings.**

light and shade

The interplay of light and shade brings life to the garden and influences its mood. Light changes constantly during the day, sometimes subtly and sometimes dramatically. Without this variation the garden would be a less intriguing place and much of its magic would be lost.

Our eyes continually adjust to light, which means that we are not always aware of how altered a view or even a solitary flower can look in differing light conditions. In the peaceful garden it is helpful to observe these changes; it is a pleasant activity and the understanding you gain may lead you to make alterations or improvements. Watch how light filters through plants onto the ground below, creating shadow patterns; lie on your back under a tree and see how sunlight illuminates the leaves; or sit next to a pond and notice the play of light on water. If you have never consciously noticed these things before it will be a revelation. Use a camera as an impartial observer – photographs taken of the same scene throughout the day will reveal just how much light affects the results.

As the sun moves across the garden the quality of light undergoes many transformations. At dawn the light is soft and diffuse, starting quite cold and grey and warming as the sun rises. This is the favourite time of day for professional garden photographers – plants are fresh and often dew-laden and there are no strong contrasts or shadows. By noon, with the sun at its highest point, the garden is full of light and shade. In direct light only strongly coloured plants can stand the competition; others tend to look bleached or dulled. Shady areas lack definition, and here it is the pale colours that stand out from the crowd. With the approach of evening, shadows lengthen and the light softens once more, bathing the garden in a golden glow before fading to darkness.

left **Attractive glass lanterns are suspended at different levels from the branch of a tree, softly illuminating their surroundings. In the absence of specially designed glass lanterns, ordinary jam jars containing candles or night lights can be hung from wires to create a similar effect.**

right **By twining pin-prick lights through a dark-leaved violet the colouring and droplets of moisture are brought into focus.**

far right **Torches are a wonderful way to light a garden on a special occasion. Pushed in among plants they can mark a path or simply act as decorations. Don't place them too close to path edges where clothing might catch light.**

Arranging your garden so that it makes the best possible use of any light will make it a more welcoming place.

The time of year and weather conditions also affect the quality of light. Even on a cloudy day there are variations – with thick cloud cover, the garden appears flat and one-dimensional, but as the cloud thins, shafts of light or dappling bring it back to life. In hot weather or where pollution is a problem the light is often hazy, while in sunny winter weather or after rain it can be crystal clear.

We cannot control the seasons or the weather, but light and shade can make a positive contribution to the garden. In the same way that lighting varies in a room – bright light for general use and soft light for intimate corners – arranging your garden so that it makes the best possible use of any light will make it a more welcoming place. A shady garden is more inviting when pools of dappled light illuminate its furthest reaches – they draw you towards them and give added depth. In the absence of direct light, a similar effect can be achieved with variegated foliage or white flowers. Conversely, sunny gardens need areas of shade for definition.

above **Light filtering through a corkscrew willow creates a delicate tracery pattern on the water in a shallow galvanized trough. The stones highlight a subtle composition that might otherwise go unnoticed.**

right **The stone table on this terrace provides a cool, shady place to eat outdoor meals during the day. When evening comes the lanterns hanging above the table are lit to make the perfect spot to enjoy an alfresco dinner.**

Light and shade are not only about how the garden looks, they are also about how it feels – in other words warmth and coolness. In a predominantly shady garden it is nice to have a patch of sun to bask in, and in a sunny garden the shade of a tree is a welcome retreat from soaring summer temperatures. These days most of us are more careful about exposure to the direct sun, especially around noon, but it is always pleasant to have somewhere to sit that catches the early morning or evening sun, even if it isn't close to the house. A distant bench positioned to catch the last rays of the setting sun will lure you outside to enjoy the peace and quiet of the garden. What better way to switch off after a hard day's work?

A distant bench positioned to catch the last rays of the setting sun will lure you outside to enjoy the peace and quiet of the garden. What better way to switch off after a hard day's work?

left **The play of light on the water of this natural stone swimming pool is far more enticing than it would be on a more conventional tiled pool. Areas of sun and shade around the pool provide relaxing spots for both sun-worshippers and shade-lovers alike.**

above left **A rustic lantern provides subtle lighting for a romantic outdoor dinner.**

above right **Perfectly positioned to catch the setting sun, this summerhouse is the ideal place to retreat to at the end of the day to enjoy a spell of peace and quiet.**

When buying a new home it is always worth asking the vendors where the sun rises and sets. Better still, try and visit the property at different times of day so that you can observe the light for yourself. When I bought my house, it wasn't until I moved in that I realized that, because it is situated on the wooded western slope of a valley, it loses the sun quite early in the evening. This means that it is wonderfully sheltered from the prevailing winds, but I do miss wandering round the garden in the warm evening sunshine.

Lanterns, candles, torches and fairy lights can be used to light alfresco meals or give the garden atmosphere on special occasions.

The night-time garden is a place of darkness and mystery, so maybe it isn't surprising that many people are reluctant to venture out into their gardens after dark, even though they are so familiar during the day. Unfortunately the only artificial lighting that exists in most gardens is for security purposes, and it is about as flattering to its surroundings as the lighting in multi-storey car parks. Although installing well-designed garden lighting is quite an expensive process, its transforming effect is worth every penny. It can make an ordinary garden look quite magical, with washes and pools of light making the familiar seem quite new, and will greatly extend the time you spend outdoors. Expert advice is to be recommended as this is a specialist subject. Solar lighting that needs no wiring is

becoming more common, but in general the lamps give off very little light and are not very attractively designed. If and when the technology and the design improve, they may open up many new possibilities for garden lighting.

On a much more modest scale, lanterns, candles, torches and fairy lights can be used to light alfresco meals or give the garden atmosphere on special occasions. Fairy lights can be twined through plants, around pergolas and up plant supports if there is an outdoor power source, but make sure you use lights that are safe outside. Floating candles transform a pond, and a candlelit table on the terrace is the perfect setting for a romantic meal. Chinese paper lanterns, hung from trees and illuminated by night lights, are both exotic and practical.

opposite left **In this Los Angeles garden, fairy lights strung through the climbing plants on the pergola echo the city lights that twinkle far below. Crystal decorations have been hung from the pergola to catch the light. Comfortable chairs complete this inviting sitting area, a perfect spot for outdoor entertaining.**

opposite right **A tiny London courtyard comes to life at night when it is lit by night lights in Moroccan tea glasses, lanterns and a shiny copper bowl.**

above **The highly burnished copper bowl glows with reflected light, amplifying the effect of the tea lights.**

right **This group of glass candle holders is both pretty and practical – the candles are safely contained and will burn better protected from any draughts. The reflection of the flames creates ever-changing patterns on the glass.**

scent and sound

fragrant plants

herbs

cool water and rustling breezes

Close your eyes in a peaceful garden and its magic
continues as your other senses are soothed and fine-
tuned. The scent of perfumed flowers and aromatic
herbs hangs in the air, and free of visual distraction,
will envelop you. As you breathe in the fragrance you
will become more aware of the soothing sounds around
you – splashing water, rustling foliage or birdsong.

fragrant plants

In our relationship with plants, fragrance is frequently as significant as appearance. There are plants of modest appearance that we grow purely for their scent – plants like mignonette, *Reseda odorata*, and night-scented stocks, *Matthiola bicornis* – while there are others that disappoint if they fail to smell as we expect. Roses or sweet peas with no scent are diminished by their lack of fragrance.

Our love affair with scented flowers has a long history. The Egyptians grew the sacred lotus for its voluptuous and narcotic scent. The Romans were so enamoured of the rose that they filled fountains with its petals, and the Persians invented the process of distillation to extract the essential oil from roses. During the Middle Ages in Europe, scented flowers were given as love tokens and some also had religious significance. The lily in particular was a symbol of fertility and purity and for centuries any painting of the Annunciation would include a lily held by the Madonna or an angel.

Our sense of smell works differently from the other senses because the olfactory nerves head straight for the

PLANTS WITH FRAGRANT FLOWERS

Winter: *Hamamelis* (witch hazel)

Sarcococca humilis

Viburnum x *bodnantense* 'Dawn'

Spring: *Convallaria majalis* (lily of the valley)

Daphne odora 'Aureomarginata'

Mahonia aquifolium (Oregon grape)

Summer: *Hesperis matronalis* (sweet rocket)

Jasmine, common or star

Lathyrus odoratus (sweet pea)

Lavandula (lavender)

Lilium candidum (Madonna lily)

Lonicera (honeysuckle)

Matthiola bicornis (night-scented stock)

Paeonia lactiflora (peony)

Philadelphus coronarius (mock orange)

Phlox paniculata (border phlox)

Reseda odorata (mignonette)

Rosa gallica var. *officinalis* and others

emotions. Scent and memory are inextricably entangled, and a familiar fragrance will always recall past events. If you first smelled lavender in your grandmother's garden on a sunny day during a happy childhood holiday then lavender will recreate that feeling of happiness, while a heart broken under a honeysuckle will always associate its sweet fragrance with sadness. Before planting a scented garden it is interesting to check

left In a wildflower meadow a beautiful white rose scrambles through a neighbouring tree – evidence of a long-abandoned garden.

your own responses to the plants you have in mind. Scent is so subjective that other people's recommendations are not always appropriate.

The volatile oils that give flowers their fragrance are at their most concentrated in the plant early in the day. This is why roses that are gathered for perfumes are harvested at dawn. As the sun warms the flowers the oils evaporate and the fragrance is diffused into the surrounding air. When you walk through a sunny garden enjoying its sweet scents you are literally breathing in perfumed air.

Garden scents change with the seasons. Even in midwinter fragrant plants perfume the air. Witch hazel will stop you in your tracks, as will the scent of winter-flowering *Viburnum* and *Sarcococca*. Plant them close to a well-used path or terrace, unless you are in the habit of wandering round the garden in midwinter. In early spring the Oregon grape *Mahonia* and *Daphne odora* 'Aureomarginata' are deliciously scented, while lily of the valley is best picked and brought indoors to appreciate its lovely perfume. There are of course plenty of scented bulbs too – daffodils, jonquils, narcissus, hyacinths, and there are even tulips that have a sweet freesia scent, 'Ballerina' being one of the finest.

Once the summer arrives there are so many fragrances to choose from – the bubble-gum scent of the mock orange, the citrus scent of peony flowers, the musky fragrance of border phlox. As at the perfume counter of a department store you can take your pick of everything from the subtle to the overpowering.

Scented flowers are best appreciated in a sunny, sheltered garden – the sun concentrates

above **The pink and white blooms of this old-fashioned sweet pea are quite small but intensely fragrant. Fortunately many of the larger-flowered modern sweet peas are now having fragrance bred back into them, but it is always worth adding a few old varieties as well. To appreciate the scent of sweet peas you really need to grow them yourself – once picked the fragrance fades.**

right **Not all roses have a fine scent. The 'Peace' rose may have a perfect, delicate beauty, but sadly its fragrance does not match its looks.**

far right **Like a parfumier, the gardener can combine scented plants so that their different aromas blend into a delicious fragrance. In this garden, honeysuckle, roses and lilies combine together in a heady perfume.**

the oils and shelter ensures that the scent hangs in the air rather than being blown away by the wind. The effect can be accentuated further by growing plants over bowers, arbours, arches and pergolas – all of which will trap the scent within them. A mixture of roses, honeysuckle, and jasmines – both *Jasminum officinale*, common jasmine, and the star jasmine, *Trachelospermum jasminoides*, will provide long-lasting fragrance. Although their season is quite short, scented wisterias have a dramatic beauty, especially when the blooms hang down within a pergola. On a pathway fringed with fragrant plants, allow them to fall across its margins so that you brush against them and release their fragrance.

Of all scented flowers, roses are probably the most universally popular, but there is an enormous variability in their scent as well as their other qualities. The four roses considered best for the making of rose oil, and therefore the most fragrant, are 'Belle de Crécy', 'Louise Odier', 'Madame Isaac Pereire' and 'Roseraie de l'Haÿ', but it is worth remembering that these old varieties are not always repeat flowering and they can have rather untidy habits. Many modern roses are now bred to have the virtues of good scent, good growth habit and disease resistance.

Lavender is the quintessential cottage garden flower, but it needs the right conditions to grow well. It is a Mediterranean plant, so give it the full sun and good drainage it loves and it will thrive. It isn't the cold that kills lavender during the winter – it's the combination of cold and wet that is lethal. 'Hidcote' is the most popular variety – its deep colour and compact habit make it ideal for lining paths and growing in containers.

Scented flowers are best appreciated in a sunny, sheltered garden – the sun concentrates the oils and shelter ensures that the scent hangs in the air rather than being blown away by the wind. Grow plants over bowers, arbours, arches and pergolas to trap the scent.

opposite **The flower of the French lavender** *Lavandula stoechas* **is very different in appearance to common lavender, but has a similar fragrance. 'Helmsdale' is a new cultivar with a striking dark burgundy flower.**

above **A rose-covered arch and a lavender-lined pathway lead to a rustic bench – the perfect place to sit and drink in the scents that surround you.**

right **A grass path leads down the centre of a fragrant lavender walk. To keep it looking this good it is essential to trim the lavender as soon as the flowers start to fade – otherwise gaps will open up in the bushes and they will start to look leggy. Lavender is relatively short-lived, so it is a good idea to take cuttings from the second year onwards. You can never have too many lavender plants.**

herbs

Herbs are perfect companions in the peaceful garden. Their reassuring presence and aromatic qualities hark back to times when we had a much more direct connection with the plants we grew – they were our food and our medicine. For many of us herbs are now the only useful plants that we still cultivate and use as an everyday ingredient.

We respond very positively to the word 'herb', as indeed we do to many of the properties of the herbs themselves – for centuries they have been used to heal, soothe, cleanse and calm, as well as being essential and much-loved flavourings in our food. Our relationship with them is often reflected in their folk names – names like bee balm (*Melissa officinalis*), knitbone (*Symphytum officinale*), eyebright (*Euphrasia officinalis*), and feverfew (*Chrysanthemum parthenium*).

Although the modern herb garden is harvested mainly for culinary herbs or sometimes for ingredients used in the making of pot pourri and lavender bags, many of us also grow other herbs, a conscious or unconscious tribute to their historical importance as folk medicines. Herbs remain more than pleasantly fragrant plants that decorate our gardens and

left **Prostrate thymes and other low-growing herbs are perfect for the spaces between paving or on a terrace.**

above right **Many of the old folk cures have been proved to have real value. Sage, so named for its reputation as a herb for improving memory, is now being used in the treatment of Alzheimer's disease.**

right **Although it is a nice idea to put a chair in the middle of a carpet of herbs, do it with caution. Bees love these herbs as much as we do, so you risk being stung.**

above left **Rosemary tumbles
over terracotta pots,
conjuring up the colours
and scent of Tuscany.**

above right **The distinctive
flavour of caraway seeds
is one of those tastes that
you either love or hate.
For some it evokes
nostalgic memories
of grandma's cakes.**

opposite **A simple plank
bench is a perfect excuse
to linger among the herbs.
The fragrance is always at
its most intense after noon,
when the volatile oils have
evaporated from the herbs
into the surrounding air.**

enliven our foods. This does not mean though
that they are all equally benign, and anyone
cultivating herbs beyond the most well-known
varieties should be familiar with their properties
before doing anything other than admiring how
they grow in the garden.

If you are planning to lay out a herb plot in
your peaceful garden, it is important that you
take into account the conditions which the
different herbs require to grow well. The
Mediterranean herbs – which include sage,
rosemary, thyme, oregano and marjoram – need
really good drainage and a hot sunny position.
Think of their natural habitat – the arid, stony
coastlines and hills of France, Italy and Greece –
and you will realize that a deeply cultivated soil
is far too rich a diet for them. They also hate to
have their roots sitting in water, so lots of added
grit is essential in all but the stoniest soils.

Enjoy herbs' aromatic qualities in the garden. Plant prostrate thyme and rosemary in between paving slabs and you will release their fragrance as you walk along the path.

above left **Basil** is a quintessential summer herb, redolent of sunny days. Here purple basil grows in an old can.

above right **Thyme** flowers attract bees and other beneficial insects. Sit near a plant and you will hear it hum.

opposite above left **Culinary thyme** should always be included in a cook's herb garden. As soon as it

has finished flowering, give the plant a trim to encourage new shoots and stop it getting too leggy.

opposite below left **Creeping thyme** loves to grow in a hot, dry place where it can tumble over a wall or the edge of a container.

opposite right **Sage** is an essential culinary herb, good in meat dishes.

However, there are other herbs which welcome a moist soil and a degree of shade. Mint, parsley and lemon balm will all do better in fertile soil in a lightly shaded position. Mint and lemon balm need to be contained in some way or they will rapidly overwhelm their less rampant neighbours. Traditionally they were planted in buckets with a hole in the base. A modern equivalent is to cut the bottom out of a large pliable plastic pot, sink it in the ground with just the rim showing above soil level, and plant into this. Mint and lemon balm spread via runners along the top of the soil, so this method will keep them contained.

Even in the tiniest herb garden, try and find space for the classic culinary herbs – parsley, sage, rosemary and thyme and a standard bay tree as well. In mild areas they can all be planted in the ground; elsewhere the less hardy plants, especially the rosemary and bay, may need to be planted in pots. Always use a soil-based compost with some added grit as this is much more suitable than compost containing peat or peat substitutes, which have a tendency to dry out in summer and conversely become waterlogged in winter.

above **Sage comes in many varieties, some purely decorative and some palatable. *Salvia officinalis* is the culinary sage. This variegated form, *Salvia officinalis* 'Icterina', tastes as good as it looks. A tisane made from the leaves with added honey is good for sore throats. The petals of the flowers, removed from the leafy calyx, taste delicious.**

right **The non-flowering form of chamomile, 'Treneague', is ideal for lawns or seats. Taller growing chamomiles are cultivated for their flowers, which are used to make soothing tisanes and in other herbal remedies.**

this page **Mint is a refreshing and stimulating herb. Like sage, it comes in many varieties with different uses. While the woolly mint** (left) **can be used in the kitchen, many varieties, such as the variegated mint** (above), **tend to be too perfumed to make enjoyable eating. Mint needs regular feeding and plenty of water to keep it growing well.**

FRAGRANT HERBS

Aloysia triphylla (lemon verbena)

Anethum graveolens (dill)

Artemisia dracunculus (tarragon)

Borago officinalis (borage)

Carum carvi (caraway)

Chamaemelum nobile (chamomile)

Coriandrum sativum (coriander)

Foeniculum vulgare (fennel)

Laurus nobilis (bay)

Melissa officinalis (lemon balm)

Mentha (mint) | *Ocimum basilicum* (basil)

Origanum vulgare (marjoram)

Petroselinum (parsley)

Rosmarinus officinalis (rosemary)

Salvia officinalis (sage)

Satureja hortensis (summer savory)

Satureja montana (winter savory)

Thymus vulgaris (common thyme)

right **A perennial sweet pea twines its way through a rosemary bush. Rosemary is a highly aromatic herb, which bears its fragile blue flowers in the depths of winter. Frequent picking of the stems keeps the plant attractively bushy – left to its own devices it has a tendency to become leggy.**

far right **The feathery foliage of fennel contrasts pleasingly with the shape of the flowering thyme in the foreground. Its delicate stems rise above its surroundings, lending height to the herb bed.**

Once you have grown lemon verbena you will never want to be without it. Brush past it and the air is filled with a delicate citrus fragrance. Its leaves can be used to make a wonderfully refreshing tisane and as a flavouring in fruit salads and cakes. Although not the easiest herb to grow, once you have found a position it likes it will survive outdoors in mild areas. A sun-baked corner at the base of a wall or a hot bank with poor, dry soil is what it likes best. This is another Mediterranean herb which hates to be wet in winter. Don't prune it until the first green shoots are showing in the spring. If grown in a pot it can be left to dry right out in the greenhouse – start watering moderately when spring is well advanced.

Many herbs are equally happy among flowers, so even if you haven't got an area dedicated to herbs you can still enjoy their aromatic qualities in the peaceful garden. Plant prostrate thyme and rosemary in between paving slabs and you will release their fragrance as you walk along the path.

cool water and rustling breezes

When we include a pond, a rill or a fountain in a peaceful garden it can make us more aware of the essential role of water in our lives. As we listen to its gentle splashing or gaze into a reflecting pool the water's presence is both reassuring and calming. Breezes ripple the surface of the water and rustle through the surrounding foliage.

For those of us who live in temperate climates where rain falls regularly and there is unlimited water flowing from our taps, it is easy to forget that water is a precious and often scarce commodity in many parts of the world. Historically, gardens could only exist where there was a reliable water source or where people had learnt to control and conserve their water. When the great gardens of the past were laid out, the control of water was frequently a central theme. The Persians piped water from distant mountains to make the desert bloom in gardens where splashing fountains and gently flowing rills cooled the dry air. In England the aristocracy and wealthy landowners employed the likes of Capability Brown and Humphrey Repton to manipulate the landscape, damming rivers and employing many hundreds of workers over decades to dig ornamental lakes or create canals. In the gardens of

above left **The seat built into the bank next to this pond is an invitation to sit down and enjoy the view. The fountain could be improved – oddly positioned and standing proud of the water, it detracts from rather than adds to the scene. There are better ways to produce the sound of splashing water.**

right **Carefully placed rocks and naturalistic planting, which includes** *Iris pseudacorus* **'Variegata' in the foreground, create the illusion of a stream tumbling down a hillside.**

A great benefit of water in the garden is the wildlife it attracts – dragonflies that hover above the water with their iridescent wings, birds that drink and bathe in it, small mammals that visit, amphibians that take up residence and tiny water-boatmen that scoot over the surface.

above **This dark, rectangular pond needs no embellishment. Its magnificent setting and its reflective qualities have a restrained perfection.**

right **It isn't always necessary to re-landscape the garden in order to introduce water. A pond in a pot in a tiny garden conjures up the feeling of an inviting jungle pool, surrounded by rocky outcrops and lush vegetation.**

right **In a contemporary garden that is
severely architectural an alcove in the wall
contains the simplest of water features.
Water splashes down into a rectangular
trough from a spout set in the wall and
then overflows into a lower pool. In a
garden devoid of natural shade this
cool corner must be a welcome relief.**

Versailles, Villa d'Este and Chatsworth, water
engineering reached its zenith with the creation
of magnificent cascades and fountains. In these
gardens water was more important than plants.

Today water is generally used on a more
modest scale, even in public spaces. We all have
the technology, most of us have sufficient water,
and with nothing to prove it seems that many of
us are content to restrict the water in our
gardens to little more than an outside tap and a
hosepipe or occasionally a concealed irrigation
system. Expense is, understandably, an
important consideration. Unless you are
fortunate enough to have natural water running
through your garden the addition of all but the
most modest of ponds is going to involve major
landscaping work. It is wise to consult an expert
in these matters – a poorly designed water
feature is worse than none at all, especially in a
peaceful garden where all the elements should
induce calm rather than irritation. Ponds that are
too shallow cause the most problems. They have
a tendency to turn green at the drop of a hat and
rapidly fill with great curtains of algae
encouraged by the warm, shallow water.
Overhanging trees that drop their leaves will clog
and pollute a pond – admittedly water can look

very pretty in a shady spot, but such a pond will need netting in autumn and regular cleaning or it will degenerate into a smelly, stagnant bog.

As with other design aspects of the peaceful garden, the way water is used should be appropriate to the setting. A formal symmetrical garden requires a formal pond. Traditional materials that echo existing features are a safe bet, but providing the shape and the dimensions are right the use of contemporary materials can offer a more interesting solution. Simple, clean lines work best in a modern urban garden where the inclusion of falling or running water effectively masks the sound of traffic and freshens the air. In a country garden, a natural pond will blend into the landscape and look

as if it has always been there. This type of pond takes time to establish and balance, but it is worth the effort and is ultimately a far more attractive solution than digging a hole and installing a preformed pond bought at a garden centre. For some unfathomable reason they are generally bright blue and strangely amoebic in shape, and it is hard to imagine any location where one would look appropriate.

Before embarking on any water feature it is essential to consider safety. If small children regularly use or visit the garden, open water of any description is potentially dangerous. There will be little enjoyment if you have to be constantly on guard to avert tragedy. This does not mean though that water must be entirely excluded – a pebble

fountain is a simple and safe way of introducing water into a small garden, or better still a water spout coming out of a wall and falling through a grating or onto stones at ground level is both safe and entertaining for children.

One of the great benefits of having water in the garden is the wildlife that it attracts – the dragonflies that hover above the water with their iridescent wings, the birds that drink and bathe in it, small mammals that visit, amphibians that take up residence and the tiny water-boatmen that scoot across the surface. If you need an excuse to linger in your peaceful garden these

above A sheet of reeded stainless steel provides a textured surface down which the water can flow, creating bubbles and movement in the water to keep the fish healthy.

left A basement area outside a townhouse has been turned from a dingy, unattractive and unused space into a Japanese-inspired water garden. Underwater lighting has been set into the trough, so its calming presence is not overlooked in the evening. Materials are thoroughly urban and the planting is simple – bamboo, cotoneaster and an arum lily.

creatures will provide it. Natural ponds provide the best environment with their shallow, gently sloping sides where marginal plants soften the edges and provide suitable wildlife habitats. A comfortable seat nearby will encourage you to sit and watch the life of the pond, and if the pond is large enough a rowing boat will allow a closer look.

Swimming pools can be a blot on the landscape, but a new development with its roots in Europe is set to change their appearance and their environmental impact in a dramatic way. Swimming ponds originated in Austria, where designers were looking for a way to make swimming pools wildlife friendly and less obtrusive. A central swimming pool is enclosed in an open tank, the top of which is just below water level, and this is surrounded by a gently sloping pond twice the size of the swimming area. Both pool and pond are lined with a dark, heavy-duty butyl liner. The pond is then lined with a deep layer of gravel and planted with a wide variety of aquatic and marginal plants, which act as oxygenators and water purifiers, doing away with the need for a filtration system. Once the swimming pond has settled down and plants are growing well there is little maintenance involved and wildlife and humans co-exist happily in

above left **Water dribbles gently over these stones through a pipe inserted in a hole drilled through the stack. Even when the water isn't flowing, they have a sculptural quality.**

below left **A large ceramic bowl has been made into an eye-catching illuminated water feature.**

right **Glass bricks were used to make this unusual water trough on a London roof terrace. Filled with pebbles, and with water splashing from above, there is not a plant in sight, but nonetheless there is a pleasant contrast of shapes and textures in the arrangement.**

their different areas of the pond. A jetty leads from the bank to the central swimming pool where you can enjoy all the best aspects of swimming in natural water without scraping your knees on concealed rocks or getting entangled in weed.

Sympathetic planting around the margins of any pool or pond adds immeasurably to the atmosphere. Waterlilies love deep, still water and are suitable for both formal and natural ponds. Marginal plants grow best in the shallows, where their roots are in wet or boggy ground and their leaves and flowers are in the sun. As well as flowering plants such as arum lilies, candelabra primulas, astilbes, and Siberian irises there are foliage plants to sway in the breezes moving across the pond.

The way water is used should be appropriate to the setting. Simple, clean lines work best in a modern urban garden where the inclusion of falling or running water effectively masks the sound of traffic and freshens the air. In a country garden, a natural pond will blend in and look as if it has always been there.

It is possible to create the illusion of flowing water in a garden with a still pond or even one with no water at all, using the sound of the wind rustling through leaves. In France, the wind blowing through the tall stands of poplar trees that punctuate the landscape sounds exactly like a rapidly flowing river. The giant grass *Arundo donax* and bamboos catch the breeze and emulate the sound of a babbling brook.

The sounds of plants are all around us once we have tuned in to them. I can stand in my own very sheltered garden with barely a zephyr ruffling my hair while the sound of the wind roars through the trees on the rim of the valley, wondering at the power of nature. Closer in, on a much smaller scale, I can hear the gentle popping of seedheads on a *Geranium palmatum* as it disperses its seeds, the rustle of dry leaves underfoot, and in the potager the gentle clatter of ripening runner-bean pods as they rattle against one another. These small, intimate sounds help focus the mind and sharpen the senses.

Some sounds are so slight that they are barely audible, but when combined with movement even they become apparent. This is particularly true with ornamental grasses – their gentle rustling could go entirely unnoticed, but the swaying of the leaves draws the eye and encourages closer examination. These small discoveries and pleasures contain within them the essential elements that can make any garden a peaceful place and a personal sanctuary.

above far left **Bamboo looks wonderful
close to ponds or streams, where the
rustling of the wind in their foliage adds
atmosphere. Select the variety carefully, as
many are rampant and their sharp shoots
can pierce the strongest of pond liners.**

above centre **Ornamental grasses, like
this *Stipa tenuissima* planted among pink
astrantias, pick up every breeze and bring
movement to the garden.**

right **From left to right, the bamboos
Phyllostachys aurea 'Holochrysa', *P. aurea*
and *P. aurea* 'Koi' have contrasting stems
and leaves. In a garden without water, the
sound of the breeze rippling through their
leaves creates the illusion of its presence.**

Architects, designers and nurseries whose work and gardens are featured in this book:

Key: a=above, b=below, c=centre, l=left, r=right

Bedmar & Shi Designers Pte Ltd
12a Keong Saik Road
Singapore 089119
t. +65 22 77117
f. +65 22 77695
*A Singapore-based firm
established in 1980, specializing
in residential projects and also in
interior design, mainly for
restaurants and offices.*
Pages 15, 38–39, 87, 131.

Jonathan Bell
11 Sinclair Gardens
London W14 0AU
t. 020 7371 3455
e. jb@jbell.demon.co.uk
Pages 18–19, 48, 86.

Susan Berger & Helen Phillips
Town Garden Design
69 Kingsdown Parade
Bristol BS6 5UG
t./f. 0117 942 3843
Pages 26–27, 47.

Tania Compton
e. taniacompton@madasafish.com
Pages 40–41, 52–53.

Cooper/Taggart Designs
t. +1 323 254 3048
e. coopertaggart@earthlink.net
Pages 88r, 106l.

De Brinkhof Garden and Nursery
Dorpsstrat 46
6616 AJ Hernen
Holland
t. +31 487 531 486
*Nursery and garden open Friday
and Saturday from 10am to 5pm,
from April until the end of
September.
A small nursery specializing in
old-fashioned and unusual
varieties of hardy perennial.*
Pages 13, 21, 34–35, 44b,
46a, 105r.

Pierre & Sandrine Degrugillier
Le Mas de Flore
Lagnes 84800
France
t. +33 04 90 20 37 96
*Antique and made-to-order
furniture.*
Page 98.

Great Dixter Nurseries
Northiam
Rye
East Sussex TN31 6PH
t. 01797 253107
f. 01797 252879
e. greatdixter@compuserve.com
Page 42.

Isabelle C. Greene, F.A.S.L.A.
Isabelle Greene & Associates
2613 De la Vina Street
Santa Barbara
CA 93105
USA
t. +1 805 569 4045
e. icgreene@aol.com
*Landscape architects and land
planners.*
Page 14.

Gruga Park Botanic Gardens
Kulshammerweg 32
D 451
49 Essen
Germany
Page 34.

HDRA's Yalding Organic Gardens
Yalding Organic Gardens
Benover Road
Yalding, near Maidstone
Kent ME18 6EX
t. 01622 814650
www.hdra.org.uk
*HDRA (Henry Doubleday Research
Association), the Organic
Association-registered charity
researching and promoting
organic gardening, farming
and food. Open 10am to 5pm
Wednesday to Sunday, May to
September, weekends only during
April and October. Also open
Easter and all Bank Holiday
Mondays.*
Page 117l.

Judy M. Horton Garden Design
136 1/2 North Larchmont
Boulevard, Suite B
Los Angeles
CA 9004
USA
t. +1 323 462 1412
f. +1 323 462 8979
e. info@jmhgardendesign.com
Pages 2, 28, 88l.

Jan Howard
Room in the Garden
Oak Cottage
Furzen Lane
Ellens Green, Rudgwick
West Sussex RH12 3AR
t. 01403 823958
*Manufacturers of elegant designs
in rusted iron. Garden design
services by Jan Howard.
Catalogue available.*
Page 62l.

Ivan Hicks
t./f. 01963 210886
e. ivan@theedge88.fsnet.co.uk
*Garden and landscape designer,
land artist.*
Pages 58l, 62r.

Iden Croft Herbs
Staplehurst
Kent
www.herbs-uk.com
Pages 59, 67, 69a, 77, 110–111,
114–115, 116, 120–121.

Japanese Garden & Bonsai
Nursery
St Mawgan
Cornwall
t. 01637 860116
Pages 45, 129.

Johnson-Naylor Interior
Architecture
t. 020 7490 8885
Pages 4r, 17, 24–25, 48–49, 83r,
89l, 102.

Judy Kameon
Elysian Landscapes
724 Academy Road
Los Angeles
CA 90012
USA
t. +1 323 226 9588
f. +1 323 226 1191
www.plainair.com
*Garden design and outdoor
furniture.*
Page 134b.

La Bambouserie de Prafrance
301040 par Anduze
France
t. +33 68 61 70 47
Pages 108, 137.

Peter & Pam Lewis
Sticky Wicket
Buckland Newton
Dorchester
Dorset DT2 7BY
t./f. 01300 345476
*Garden design, restoration and
management.*
Pages 8–9, 22l, 23, 36–37,
64–65, 112–113, 136–137.

Dale Loth Architects
1 Cliff Road
London NW1 9AJ
t. 020 7485 4003
f. 020 7284 4490
e. mail@dalelotharchitects.co.uk
Pages 132–133.

Christina Oates
Secret Garden Designs
Fovant Hut
Fovant, nr. Salisbury
Wiltshire SP3 5LN
t. 01722 714756
www.secretgardendesigns.co.uk
*Garden designer Christina Oates
specializes in imaginative and yet
down-to-earth consultancy visits
and concept plans.*
Pages 10, 44ar, 69b, 73.

Sarah Raven's Cutting Garden
Perch Hill Farm
Brightling, Robertsbridge
East Sussex TN32 5HP
t. 01424 838181
f. 01424 838571
e. info@thecuttinggarden.com
www.thecuttinggarden.com
Page 66.

Michael Reeves Interiors
33 Mossop Street
London SW3 2NB
t. 020 7225 2501
f. 020 7225 3060
Pages 84–85.

Suzanne Rheinstein Associates
817 North Hilldale Avenue
West Hollywood
CA 90069
USA
t. +1 323 931 340

and Hollyhock Hilldale
Address as above
Garden antiques and accessories.
e. Hollyhockinc@aol.com
Pages 2, 28, 81l.

Rowden Gardens
Brentor
nr. Tavistock
Devon PL19 0NG
t./f. 01822 810275
Page 81.

Marc Schoellen
35 route de Colmar-Berg
L-7525 Mersch
Grand-Duché de Luxembourg
t. +352 327 269
*Garden historian and amateur
garden designer.*
Pages 25, 68, 70, 80–81b.

Roberto Silva
128 Hemingford Road
London N1 1DE
t. 020 7700 7484
e. landrob7@aol.com
Pages 3, 20–21, 58r, 82, 90l.

Enrica Stabile
l'Utile e il Dilettevole
via Della Spiga 46
20121 Milan
Italy
t. +39 02 76004820
www.utile-delettevole.it
*Antique furniture, garden furniture,
decorative objects, soft
furnishings, textiles.*
Pages 7, 57a, 98, 100, 103, 104.

Sally Storey
John Cullen Lighting
585 Kings Road
London SW6 2EH
t. 020 7371 5400
*A wide range of practical
contemporary light fittings as well
as innovative made-to-measure
lighting design.*
Pages 16–17, 134a.

Derry Watkins
Special Plants
Greenways Lane
Cold Ashton
Chippenham
Wiltshire SN14 8LA
t. 01225 891686
e. specialplants@bigfoot.com
www.specialplants.net
*Opening hours 10.30am to
4.30pm March to September,
other times by arrangement; mail
order September to March only;
please send five second class
stamps for catalogue.*
Page 128.

Whitelaw Turkington Landscape
Architects
t. 020 7820 0388
Pages 4r, 17, 24–25, 48–49, 83r,
89l, 102.

Stephen Woodhams
378 Brixton Road
London SW9 7AW
t. 020 7346 5656
Page 135.

Picture credits

All photography by Melanie Eclare unless stated otherwise.
Key: a=above, b=below, r=right, l=left, c=centre, ph = photographer

Front endpapers: left ph Jan Baldwin, centre & right ph Andrea Jones;
2 garden of interior designer Suzanne Rheinstein, designed by Judy M.
Horton; 3 a garden in south London designed by Roberto Silva; 4l Niall
Manning & Alastair Morton's garden, Dunard, Fintry, Scotland G63 0EX;
4c ph Pia Tryde; 4r Fiona Naylor and Peter Marlow's roof garden in
London designed by Fiona Naylor and landscape architect Lindsey
Whitelaw; 5 ph Pia Tryde; 7 ph Christopher Drake/Enrica Stabile's house,
Le Thor, Provence; garden bench & cushions, l'Utile e il Dilettevole; 8–9
Sticky Wicket wildlife garden near Dorchester, designed and created by
Peter and Pam Lewis; 10 Fovant Hut Garden near Salisbury in Wiltshire
was created by garden designer Christina Oates together with her
husband Nigel and is open to the public; 12 Connie Haydon's garden in
Dorset; 13 the garden and nursery De Brinkhof of Riet Brinkhof and Joop
Van Den Berk; 14 Carol Valentine's garden in California, designed by
Isabelle Greene, F.A.S.L.A., a California landscape architect and planner;
15 ph Andrew Wood/'Melwani House' designed by Bedmar & Shi
designers in Singapore; 16–17 a house in Chelsea, lighting designed by
Sally Storey; 17 Fiona Naylor and Peter Marlow's roof garden in London
designed by Fiona Naylor and landscape architect Lindsey Whitelaw;
18–19 a garden in London designed by Jonathan Bell; 20–21 a garden in
south London designed by Roberto Silva; 21 the garden and nursery De
Brinkhof of Riet Brinkhof and Joop Van Den Berk; 22l Sticky Wicket
wildlife garden near Dorchester, designed and created by Peter and Pam
Lewis; 22r Niall Manning and Alastair Morton's garden, Dunard, Fintry,
Scotland G63 0EX; 23 Sticky Wicket wildlife garden near Dorchester,
designed and created by Peter and Pam Lewis; 24–25 Fiona Naylor and
Peter Marlow's roof garden in London designed by Fiona Naylor and
landscape architect Lindsey Whitelaw; 25 Marc Schoellen's garden in
Luxembourg called 'La Bergerie'; 26–27 the garden of James Morris in
Bristol designed by Sue Berger & Helen Phillips; 28 garden of interior
designer Suzanne Rheinstein, designed by Judy M. Horton; 29 Jim
Reynolds's garden 'Butterstream', Co. Meath, Ireland; 30 Connie Haydon's
garden in Dorset; 31 Jim Reynolds's garden 'Butterstream', Co. Meath,
Ireland; 32l Niall Manning & Alastair Morton's garden, Dunard, Fintry,
Scotland G63 0EX; 32r Jim Reynolds's garden 'Butterstream', Co. Meath,
Ireland; 33 Niall Manning & Alastair Morton's garden, Dunard, Fintry,
Scotland G63 0EX; 34 ph Andrea Jones/Gruga Park Botanic Gardens;
34–35 the garden and nursery De Brinkhof of Riet Brinkhof and Joop Van
Den Berk; 36–37 Sticky Wicket wildlife garden near Dorchester, designed
and created by Peter and Pam Lewis; 38–39 ph Andrew Wood/'Melwani
House' designed by Bedmar & Shi designers in Singapore; 40–41 Peter
and Sandra Aitken-Quack's garden at Ham Cross Farm near Tisbury,
designed by Tania Compton; 42 ph Andrea Jones/Great Dixter Nurseries;
43 ph Caroline Hughes/John and Joan Ward's garden in London; 44al
Jim Reynolds's garden 'Butterstream', Co. Meath, Ireland; 44ar Fovant Hut
Garden near Salisbury in Wiltshire was created by garden designer
Christina Oates together with her husband Nigel and is open to the public;
44b the garden and nursery De Brinkhof of Riet Brinkhof and Joop Van
Den Berk; 45 ph Andrea Jones/Japanese Garden & Bonsai Nursery; 46a
the garden and nursery De Brinkhof of Riet Brinkhof and Joop Van Den
Berk; 46b Mr. and Mrs. James Hepworth's garden in Herefordshire; 47 the
garden of James Morris in Bristol designed by Sue Berger & Helen Phillips;
48 a garden in London designed by Jonathan Bell; 48–49 Fiona Naylor
and Peter Marlow's roof garden in London designed by Fiona Naylor and
landscape architect Lindsey Whitelaw; 50 Mr. and Mrs. James Hepworth's
garden in Herefordshire; 51 ph Polly Wreford/Mary Foley's house in
Connecticut; 52–53 Peter and Sandra Aitken-Quack's garden at Ham
Cross Farm near Tisbury, designed by Tania Compton; 54 Jim Reynolds's
garden 'Butterstream', Co. Meath, Ireland; 54–55 ph Chris Tubbs/
Maureen Kelly's house in the Catskills, New York; 56 the Farrell family,
Woodnewton; 57b ph Pia Tryde; 57a Christopher Drake/Enrica Stabile's
house, Le Thor, Provence; garden bench & cushions, l'Utile e il Dilettevole;
58l Mart Barlow's garden designed by Ivan Hicks; 58r a garden in south
London designed by Roberto Silva; 59 ph Caroline Hughes/Iden Croft
Herbs; 60 Hutton Wilkinson's garden designed by Tony Duquette; 61l
Mirabel Osler's garden in Ludlow, Shropshire; 61r Hutton Wilkinson's
garden designed by Tony Duquette; 62l Jan Howard's garden in Sussex;
62r Mart Barlow's garden designed by Ivan Hicks; 63 Mirabel Osler's
garden in Ludlow, Shropshire; 64–65 Sticky Wicket wildlife garden near
Dorchester, designed and created by Peter and Pam Lewis; 66 Sarah
Raven's Cutting Garden in Brightling, designed by Sarah Raven; 67 ph
Caroline Hughes/Iden Croft Herbs; 68 Marc Schoellen's garden, 'La
Bergerie', in Luxembourg; 69a ph Caroline Hughes/Iden Croft Herbs; 69b
Fovant Hut Garden near Salisbury in Wiltshire was created by garden

designer Christina Oates together with her husband Nigel and is open to the public; **70** Marc Schoellen's garden, 'La Bergerie', in Luxembourg; **72b** ph Francesca Yorke; **73** Fovant Hut Garden near Salisbury in Wiltshire was created by garden designer Christina Oates together with her husband Nigel and is open to the public; **74r** ph Pia Tryde; **75** ph Francesca Yorke; **76al** ph Caroline Hughes; **76bl & r** ph Andrea Jones; **77** ph Caroline Arber/Rosemary Titterington at Iden Croft Herbs; **78al** ph Chris Tubbs; **78bl, br & 79a** ph Pia Tryde; **79b** ph Andrea Jones; **80l** ph Pia Tryde; **80ar** ph Andrea Jones; **80–81b** Marc Schoellen's garden, 'La Bergerie', in Luxembourg; **81** ph Andrea Jones/Rowden Gardens; **82** a garden in south London designed by Roberto Silva; **83al** ph Andrew Wood; **83r both** Fiona Naylor and Peter Marlow's roof garden in London designed by Fiona Naylor and landscape architect Lindsey Whitelaw; **84–85** ph Catherine Gratwicke/Marja Walters – London, designed by Michael Reeves, Kauna mats from Ganesha, bamboo table from Emily Readett-Bayley, linen towels from Eastern Trading Allowance; **86** a garden in London designed by Jonathan Bell; **87** ph Andrew Wood/'Melwani House' designed by Bedmar & Shi designers in Singapore; **88l** garden of interior designer Suzanne Rheinstein, designed by Judy M. Horton; **88r** Laura Cooper and Nick Taggart's Los Angeles garden, designed by Cooper/Taggart Designs; **89l** Fiona Naylor and Peter Marlow's roof garden in London designed by Fiona Naylor and landscape architect Lindsey Whitelaw; **89r** ph Andrea Jones/Stoners; **90l** a garden in south London designed by Roberto Silva; **90–91 & 91c** ph Caroline Hughes/John and Joan Ward's garden in London; **91r** Mr. and Mrs. James Hepworth's garden in Herefordshire; **92–93** all ph Andrea Jones; **94** ph Chris Tubbs; **96r & 97** © ph Steve Painter; **98** ph Christopher Drake/Mr. & Mme. Degrugillier, Le Mas de Flore, Antiquite et Creation, Lagnes, Isle sur Sorgue, Provence; garden table & chair, Le Mas de Flore; cushion, l'Utile e il Dilettevole; **99** ph Andrea Jones; **100** ph Christopher Drake/antique lanterns, l'Utile e il Dilettevole; **100–101** Elspeth Thompson's garden in south London; **101** ph Christopher Drake/Guido & Marilea Somarè's house in Milan; bamboo garden lamps, Habitat; **102** Fiona Naylor and Peter Marlow's roof garden in London designed by Fiona Naylor and landscape architect Lindsey Whitelaw; **103** ph Christopher Drake/Enrica Stabile's house in Provence; **104** ph Christopher Drake/Giorgio & Irene Silvagni's house in Provence; iron bed by Giorgio Silvagni at L'Utile e il

Dilettevole; silk moiré cushion, L'Utile e il Dilettevole; **105l** ph Tom Leighton; **105r** the garden and nursery De Brinkhof of Riet Brinkhof & Joop Van Den Berk; **106l** Laura Cooper & Nick Taggart's Los Angeles garden designed by Cooper/Taggart Designs; **106r & 107l** Elspeth Thompson's garden in south London; **107r** ph Pia Tryde; **108** ph Andrea Jones/La Bambouserie de Prafrance; **110–111** ph Caroline Hughes/Iden Croft Herbs; **112–113** Sticky Wicket wildlife garden near Dorchester, designed and created by Peter and Pam Lewis; **114** ph Stephen Robson; **114–115** ph Caroline Hughes/Iden Croft Herbs; **115** ph Stephen Robson; **116** ph Caroline Hughes/Iden Croft Herbs; **117l** ph Caroline Hughes/HDRA's Yalding Organic Gardens, near Maidstone, Kent; **117r** ph Stephen Robson; **118** ph Anne Hyde; **119a** ph Francesca Yorke; **119b & 120l** ph Pia Tryde; **120c** ph Caroline Arber; **120–121** ph Caroline Hughes/Iden Croft Herbs; **122–127** ph Caroline Hughes; **128** Derry Watkins's garden in Wiltshire designed by Derry Watkins and her husband, the architect Peter Clegg; **129** ph Andrea Jones/Japanese Garden & Bonsai Nursery; **130l** Niall Manning & Alastair Morton's garden, Dunard, Fintry, Scotland G63 0EX; **130r** ph Jan Baldwin; **131** ph Andrew Wood/'Melwani House' designed by Bedmar & Shi designers in Singapore; **132–133** architect's house and garden in London designed by Dale Loth Architects; **134a** a house in Chelsea, lighting designed by Sally Storey; **134b** garden designed by Judy Kameon – Elysian Landscapes; **135** Sarah Harrison & Jamie Hodder-Williams's roof terrace in London designed by Stephen Woodhams; **136l** ph Andrea Jones; **136–137** Sticky Wicket wildlife garden near Dorchester, designed and created by Peter and Pam Lewis; **137** ph Andrea Jones/La Bambouserie de Prafrance; **back endpapers:** all ph Andrea Jones.

Index

Page numbers in *italic* refer to the illustrations

A

acanthus *28*
agapanthus *78*, 79
Allium 72, 73, 74, 79
   A. cristophii 23
Aloysia triphylla 126
Ammi majus 78, 79
Amsterdam 50
Anethum graveolens 126
arbours 116
arches *61, 64–5*, 66, *66*, 116, *117*
architectural plants 18, 24, 66, 91
art works 60–2, *62–3*
Artemisia 96
   A. dracunculus 126
   A. 'Powis Castle' 85
arum lilies *132–3*, 135
Arundo donax 136
Asplenium scolopendrium 97
astilbes 135
Astrantia 136–7
   A. major 78, 79
Austria 134

B

balance 29–41
balconies 53–4
Ballota pseudodictamnus 85
bamboos *34*, 66, 85, 92, 97, *132–3*, 136,
   136–7
basil *76, 122*, 126
bay trees *30, 124*, 126
bee balm 119
bees *119*
Bell, Jonathan *18*
benches *7, 32, 47, 51, 54, 57, 57, 69,*
   80, 102, *117, 120–1*
Beverly Hills 60
bishop's flower 79
blue flowers 72, 75
bold foliage 91, 92
borage 126
Borago officinalis 126
'borrowed views' 12–17
boundaries 14
box
   edging *32, 40–1*, 79
   topiary *29, 32, 33*
brick terraces *88*
Briza maxima 92
Brown, Capability 128

Buddhism 82
Buddleja alternifolia 22
bulbs, scented 114
Burnett, Frances Hodgson 62

C

candelabra primulas 135
candles 106, *107*
caraway *120*, 126
Carum carvi 126
catmint *77*, 79
Cercis siliquastrum 73
Cerinthe 79
chairs *54–5*, 57, *119*
Chamaemelum nobile 126
   C. n. 'Treneague' *124*
chamomile *36–7*, 126
Chatsworth, Derbyshire 131
children 21, 53, *132–3*
Chrysanthemum parthenium 119
city gardens 18–21, *18–19*, 53–4, 86,
   86
Clematis macropetala 72, 79
climbing plants 66
colours 40, 72–81
   colour-themed gardens *27*, 79
   light and shade 99
   simplicity 22–3, *26–7*
Compton, Tania *40–1*
containers
   as focal point 32, *32*
   miniature gardens *14*
   symmetry *30*
   on terraces 54–7
   waterlilies in 27
contemplation 42–57
Convallaria majalis 113
copper beech *31*
coriander 126
Coriandrum sativum 126
corkscrew willows *102*
cornflowers 69
cotoneaster *132–3*
cottage gardens *110–11*
cotton lavender *77*
country gardens, wild flowers 23–4
courtyards *15*, 18, *38–9, 106*
cow parsley *78*
cream flowers 72
cushions 57, *57*

D

daffodils 114
daisies *32*
Daphne odora 'Aureomarginata' 113,
   114
decking 27, *82–3, 89*
design, balanced gardens 39
Digitalis purpurea 79
   D. p. f. *albiflora* 79
dill 126
doors *59*, 62–5, *66*, 68
Dryopteris dilatata 80

E

eating areas *20–1*, 57, *103*
elaeagnus 49
Eriophorum angustifolium 79
Eryngium alpinum 85
   E. bourgatii 76, 79
Eschscholzia 85, 96
Euphrasia officinalis 119
eyebright 119

F

fairy lights *100–1*, 106, *106*
Falcon's Lair *60*
family gardens 21
Fatsia 91
fences 14, 17, *66*
fennel 85, *96*, 97, 126
ferns *80–1*, 85, 91, 96–7
   hart's-tongue *97*
Festuca glauca 92
feverfew 119
Fish, Margery 65
flag irises *78*
focal points 12
   framing *64–5*, 65
   paths 32
   symmetrical gardens 30
   in urban gardens 18
   water features 24–7, *24–5*, 32
Foeniculum vulgare 85, 126
foliage *see* leaves
formal gardens *29*, 35, 132
'found' objects 60
fountains 24, *128*, 131, *132–3, 134*
foxgloves 66, *79*, 79
fragrant plants 66, 110–17
framing views *64–5*, 65
France 136

French lavender *116*
furniture 57

G

Geranium palmatum 136
   G. phaeum 22
grasses *22*, 24, *89*, 91, *92–5, 92–3*, 136,
   136–7
gravel *16–17*, 83, *84–5*, 85, *88*
green foliage *72–5, 80–1*
Gunnera 91, 92

H

Hamamelis 113
hammocks 46, *52–3*, 53
hart's-tongue ferns 97
hedges
   balance *31, 34–5*
   framing views with 14, 17
   symmetry *32, 40–1*
Helleborus orientalis 79
herbaceous borders 13
herbs 46, 91, 119–27
Hesperis matronalis 79, 113
Hicks, Ivan *58*, 62
Holland 50, 75
honeysuckle 113, *115*, 116
Hosta 85, *89*, 91, 92, *96*
hyacinths 114
Hydrangea 79

I

illusions 32, *61*, 62
intuition 39–40
Ipomoea 79
Iris 78, 79, 135
   I. pseudacorus 'Variegata' *129*

J

Japanese-style gardens *15, 132–3*
jasmine 113, 116
Jasminum officinale 116
jetties *44*, 135
jonquils 114
Judas tree *73*

K

knapweed *93*
knitbone 119

L

lamb's ears 97
landscape, 'borrowed views' 12–17
lanterns *100*, *103*, *105*, 106, *106*
Lathyrus odoratus 113
Laurus nobilis 126
Lavandula 79, 113
  L. 'Hidcote' 116
  L. stoechas 'Helmsdale' *116*
lavender *47*, 66, 79, 113, 116, *116*, *117*,
  119
lawns 95
  chamomile *36–7*
leaves
  colour 72–5, *80–1*
  shapes 24, 88
  texture 91–2
  variegated foliage 100
lemon balm 124, 126
lemon verbena 126
Lewis, C. S. 62
Lewis, Peter and Pam *23*
light and shade 99–107
lighting *100–1*, *103*, 106, *133*
lilies 110, *115*
  canna *75*
  madonna 113
  martagon 66
Lilium candidum 113
lily of the valley 113, 114
lime trees *47*
linear foliage 91, *92–5*
London *24*, *49*, *58*, *106*, *135*
Lonicera 113
Los Angeles *106*
love-in-a-mist 79
low maintenance gardens *16–17*

M

madonna lilies 113
Mahonia 114
  M. aquifolium 113
marjoram *77*, 79, 120, 126
martagon lilies 66
Marvell, Andrew 72
masterwort 79
materials, texture 85–8
Matteuccia struthiopteris 81
Matthiola bicornis 110, 113
meadows *22*, 24, *64–5*, *112–13*
meditation 83

Mediterranean plants 120, 126
Melissa officinalis 119, 126
Mentha 126
mignonette 110, 113
miniature gardens *14*
mint 124, *125*, 126
  variegated *125*
  woolly *125*
mirrors *61*, 62
mock orange 113, 114
monastic gardens 42, 44–6, 82
Monet, Claude *42*
morning glory *74*, 79
mullein 97

N

narcissus 114
Nepeta 77, 79
Nigella 79
night lights *106–7*
night-time gardens 106

O

Ocimum basilicum 126
olive trees 69
Omar Khayyam 69
optical illusions 32, *61*, 62
orange flowers 72–5
oregano 120
Oregon grape 113, 114
Origanum 77
  O. vulgare 79, 126
Osler, Mirabel *61*

P

Paeonia lactiflora 113
palms *89*
  sago *28*
Panicum virgatum 'Shenandoah' *92*
Papaver somniferum 79, 85
parsley 124, 126
paths *12*, *66*, *80*
  balance *34–5*
  destinations 32
  perspective 32
  railway sleepers *88*
  scented plants 116, *117*
  symmetry 30
  texture *91*
  through meadows *22*, 24, *64–5*
pavilions 49–50

paving slabs, sitting areas 27
pebble fountains 132–3, *134*
pebbles *82–3*, 83, *86*, *89*, *91*
Pelargonium tomentosum 85
peonies 113, 114
pergolas *43*, 106, *106*, 116
Persian gardens 42–4, 46, 128
perspective, optical illusions 32
Petroselinum 126
Philadelphus coronarius 113
Phlox 114
  P. paniculata 113
phormiums *89*
Phyllostachys aurea 137
  P. a. 'Holochrysa' *137*
  P. a. 'Koi' *137*
physic gardens 46
pink flowers 72, 75
planning, balanced gardens 39
plants
  fragrance 110–17
  ponds 135
  shapes 24, 88
  simplicity 22–3, *22*
  special places 65–9
  textures 88–91
ponds 27, *42*, *128*, *130*, 131–6, *132–3*
  floating candles 106
  jetties *44*
  reflections *25*, *28*, 49
  wildlife ponds *45*
poplar trees 136
poppies
  California 85
  opium 79, 85
post and rail fences 14
potagers 13
Primula vialii 75
primulas, candelabra 135
privacy 14–17, 54
purple flowers 72, 75
pussy willow 85

Q

quaking grass *92*

R

railway sleepers *88*
reclamation yards 62
red flowers 72–5
reflections, ponds *25*, *28*, 49

relaxation 46–57
Repton, Humphrey 128
Reseda odorata 110, 113
Rheum 91
rills *24–5*, 27, 46
rocks, Zen gardens 82–3
Romneya coulteri 85
roof gardens 17, *48–9*, 53–4
rosemary 66, 120, *120*, 124, 126, *126*
roses (*Rosa*) *40–1*, *47*, 66, 69, 97, 110,
  110–13, 114, 116, *117*
  R. 'Belle de Crécy' 116
  R. gallica var. *officinalis* 113
  R. 'Louise Odier' 116
  R. 'Madame Isaac Pereire' 116
  R. 'Peace' *114–15*
  R. 'Roseraie de l'Haÿ' 116
Rosmarinus officinalis 126
rural gardens, wild flowers 23–4

S

safety, water 132–3
sage 85, *94*, *119*, 120, *123*, 124, *124*,
  126
sago palm *28*
Salix caprea 85
Salvia officinalis 85, 126
  S. o. 'Icterina' *124*
Santolina 77
Sarcococca 114
  S. humilis 113
Satureja hortensis 126
  S. montana 126
savory
  summer 126
  winter 126
scabious *23*
scented plants 66, 110–17
screens 17, 54
sculpture 32, *61*
sea holly 79
seating 27, 32, 57, *84–5*
  see also benches; chairs
Secret Garden, The 62
Sedum 85, 97
Senecio cineraria 96
shady gardens 66, 99–107
shapes
  leaves 24, 88
  plant outlines 24, 88
  water features 27

shrubs, Zen gardens 83
shuttlecock fern *81*
Siberian irises 135
Silva, Roberto *20–1, 58*
simplicity 12–27
Sissinghurst, Kent 79
slugs 92
Smith, Joe *63*
snails 92
solar lighting 106
Somerset 62–5
sounds 136
special places 58–69
Stachys lanata 85, 97
stained-glass panels 62
star jasmine 113, 116
statues 32, *61*
stepping stones *83*
steps *12*
Sticky Wicket, Dorset *23, 36–7*
Stipa gigantea 92
  S. tenuifolia 85
  S. tenuissima 93, 136–7
stocks, night-scented 110, 113
stone *31*, 86–8, *87, 90*
streams *129*

succulents *14, 95*
summerhouses *44, 46*, 49–50, 57, *60, 105*
sunflowers *18*
sunny gardens 102, 105, 114–16
sweet peas 110, 113, *114, 120*
sweet rocket 79, 113
swimming pools *104*, 134–5
swings *46, 50*, 53
symmetry 29–41, 42–4, 132
Symphytum officinale 119

T
tables *54–5*, 57, *84–5, 103*
tarragon 126
tea lights *106–7*
terraces 54–7, *88, 103*
textures 82–97
Thalictrum 85, 96
thyme 66, *118*, 120, *122–3*, 124, 126
Thymus vulgaris 126
topiary *29, 32, 33, 35, 68*
torches *101*, 106
Trachelospermum jasminoides 116
treehouses 50–3, *56*

trees
  as focal points *33, 64*
  framing views with 14
  in urban gardens 18, *18–19*
trellis 17, *18–19*
troughs, water *102, 131, 135*
Tulipa 'Ballerina' 114

U
urban gardens 18–21, *18–19*, 53–4, 86, *86*

V
Valentino, Rudolph *60*
variegated foliage 100
vegetable gardens *13*
verandahs *51*, 54–7
Verbascum olympicum 85, 97
Versailles 131
Viburnum 114
  V. x *bodnantense* 'Dawn' 113
views 12–17, *64–5*, 65
Villa d'Este 131
vines *43*
violets *100–1*

W
walls
  doors in *59*, 62–5, *69*
  texture *87, 90*
water features 24–7, *24–5*, 32, 44, *102*, 128–37
water spouts *131*, 133
waterlilies 27, 135
weather, light and shade 99
white flowers 66, 72, 79, 100
wild flowers 23–4, 40, *112–13*
wildlife *45*, 95, 130, 133–4
willows, corkscrew *102*
wind 18, 136
wind chimes *62*
wisteria 116
witch hazel 113, 114
woodland gardens 66, *69*
work spaces, views from 21–2, *48*

Y
yellow flowers 72–5
yucca *99*

Z
Zen gardens 42, 46, 82–5